BARBEY

BARBEY

The Story of a Pioneer
Columbia River Salmon Packer

By
Roger T. Tetlow
And
Graham J. Barbey

Binford & Mort Publishing
Portland, Oregon

CONTENTS

ACKNOWLEDGMENTS

My long journey through the days of Henry Barbey's life has finally ended with the publication of this book. It took three years and many miles of traveling to get all of the information, facts, and personal narratives I have used, and I owe a debt of gratitude to the many people I met along the way who helped me piece together the story of Henry Barbey and the Barbey Packing Co.

Even though the Columbia River salmon fishing industry is now virtually a thing of the past, there are still many individuals living who were a part of that grand and colorful time, and who remember it as if it all happened yesterday. Each one of these willingly gave of his or her time and memory to help me write this history as factually and accurately as possible.

I would like to acknowledge each of their contributions and thank these wonderful people for their time, their efforts, and their patience. I can only hope that each of them will be pleased with my efforts.

This book would not have been written if it had not been for Graham Barbey's decision to commission a book honoring his father and recording Henry Barbey's contribution to the early salmon and tuna canning industry on the Columbia River. In addition to providing hours of taped memories, he took the time to provide me with the names and addresses of relatives, ex-employees, friends, and business associates to contact for their memories of Henry Barbey. He gladly read each chapter as it was written and offered many helpful comments and friendly criticisms. He also provided most of the photographs used in this book. I can only hope that this book as I have written it has not disappointed him.

Miss Frances Barbey and her niece Carolyn Kelley generously shared with me their memories of Henry Barbey and other members of the Barbey family, and allowed me to copy many of their family photographs.

Mrs. Katherine Barbey, the widow of Admiral Barbey,

invited me to her home at Olympia, Washington, and talked with me about her late husband and other members of the Barbey family. A truly gracious lady, in addition to telling me about those long-ago days, she showed me the many medals and other mementos of Admiral Barbey's career. It was an afternoon to remember.

Clarence Sigurdson of Seaside, a born storyteller and a fine author in his own right, was kind enough to devote the better part of two days to share with me his many memories of the days he spent working for Henry Barbey at Pillar Rock and at Rabbit Island. His keen memory made it possible for me to fill in many of the gaps I had in my knowledge of these two places and the events which took place there.

For details of the life of Chesley Smith, I am indebted to Chesley A. Smith of Bainbridge Island, Washington, and Robert Smith of Reedsport, Oregon, for their recollections of their father's life and work, and for providing photographs of him. I am also indebted to Marian McMindes Smith, a former Astoria High School classmate of mine, who greatly assisted me in this task.

Herb Palmberg of Warrenton provided many of the details of Henry Barbey's purchase of his home on Jerome Street, and of other anecdotes about that period of time. I am grateful for his assistance and for devoting that amount of his time to my work.

I spent a delightful afternoon at the Clatsop Care Center at Astoria talking with Mrs. Christine Hendrickson Loback, Mrs. Esther Rinne, and Mrs. Impi Palo about the old days at the Barbey Packing Co. These gracious ladies, with their wonderful memories of those long-ago days, added life and color to my somewhat dry account of those events and times. I am sure all of the readers of this book will be delighted with their colorful stories of Henry Barbey.

Alfred Johnson of Nasel, Washington, was kind enough to invite me to his home after he heard that I was writing about Henry Barbey. His many stories of the days he spent working on the seining grounds gave me a great deal of background information on the daily routine of the men living out on the river during the fishing season.

Manuel Schnitzer of Portland remembered Henry Barbey

when he was first starting out in Portland and shared with me his memories of that time and that place.

I drove to Tacoma to interview Dorothy Caughey Johnson, long-time office worker for Henry Barbey, and found that she had been there at the same time that I worked for the Barbeys. We had a grand day sharing memories about those wonderful days. Because she had been so close to the Barbey operations, she was able to fill in many of the details of work at the Barbey cannery, and had many anecdotes to tell about the Barbeys and about other employees as well. I owe her many thanks for her help with this project.

Riphath and Nethaneel Christensen are two brothers who both live out on Tucker Creek Road near Astoria. They were kind enough to invite me to their homes to tell me about their days with the Barbey Packing Co. I had a wonderful afternoon with them, listening to their colorful accounts of those long-ago days, many of which I have used in this book.

Mrs. Joseph Knapp of Portland willingly talked about the days when she and the Barbeys were good friends and shared many good times together. I appreciate her sharing these memories with me.

Jim Ferguson of Seattle was kind enough to use part of his Thanksgiving vacation to talk with me about the days when he worked for Henry and Graham Barbey. He had a good knowledge of the later days of the packing company and contributed many anecdotes about the Barbeys which helped me write the final chapters of this book.

I never met Byron Fitzgerald of Salem, Oregon, but he was kind enough to send me several long letters giving details of his life as a Barbey employee, and also sent me most of the photos of the Sand Island seining ground which have been used in this book.

Morna Fitzgerald Raby of Sherman Oaks, Calif. sent a long letter in answer to my queries about her experiences working for the Barbey Packing Co. and filled me in on many of the details of working in the cannery office for the Barbeys.

Vern Hall of Sweet Home, Oregon, wrote several letters to me and then I had a chance later on to talk with him about his experiences with seining-ground horses. His experiences added color to the book and I thank him for helping me on this project.

Mrs. Louise Kruckman Larson of Forest Grove, Oregon, sent me information about George Kruckman, one of the pioneer seining-ground bosses. Even though he didn't work for Barbey, he does appear in one of the episodes and I am indebted to Mrs. Larson for the information and encouragement she sent in her letter.

Both Joe Bakkensen of Gearhart and Ted Bugas of Astoria took the time to talk with me about the final days of the Barbey cannery and of their participation in those fairly recent events. I appreciate both the time they gave and the information they passed on to me, and thank both of them for their courtesy.

I am in debt to both Henry Young and Eugene Sing for contributing so much to the Chinese sections of this book. I talked with both of them at different times, discussing their days at the Barbey plant and the other people they knew there. I cannot thank either of them enough for their kind assistance.

Loren Knapp of Astoria generously allowed me to use some of the Union Fish's records he has in his possession which helped make that section of the book accurate and complete.

The photographs of Rabbit Island were sent to me by D. Sutter of Arcadia, California. Their inclusion added realism and color to that portion of the book.

I am indebted to Bruce Berney of the Astor Public Library of Astoria for giving me access to the CRPA files stored there, and helping me locate other research materials.

Larry Gilmore, former curator of the Columbia River Maritime Museum was very helpful, allowing me to use many of the back issues of the various west coast fishing magazines stored there, as well as locating other Barbey materials needed in my research.

For material on Chief Charlie, I went to Noreen Robinson, director of the Ilwaco (Washington) Heritage Museum, who helped me locate photographs and clippings on this legendary Indian chief.

Without the help and encouragement I received from those individuals mentioned above and from my many friends in Astoria and the Lower Columbia area, this book would never have been written.

Thank you again.

PROLOGUE

Not too many years ago, Astoria, Oregon was the salmon canning capital of the world. The Columbia River rolled past the waterfront and, in that fast-moving mass of water, the hordes of salmon passed the town, heading up the river for their annual spawning rites. They came in the early spring and then again in the fall of the year, as regular as the tides and waves which had cradled them during the years they had spent out in the salt water of the Pacific Ocean.

Each year, the salmon came back to Astoria; the mighty Chinooks, the bright silvers, the blueback, chum, and the elusive steelhead all came back into the river they had left years before. Most of them did not pause in passing but they came in such sheer numbers that the river seemed to be alive with them.

The people of Astoria expected them and prepared to meet them out on that watery battleground in places with names like Peacock Spit, Desdemona Sands, Jim Crow Sands, and Sand Island. Some met them in small boats, trying to catch the salmon in their gillnets as they passed. Others waited by tar-covered traps built close to shore, while others went out with horses and boats, fighting the salmon on the wet sands in the middle of the river. There were others too and they met the salmon and caught them or lost them as chance dictated.

The people of Astoria — the Finns, Norwegians, Swedes, and all the others of divergent nationalities and races — were ready for the salmon because they knew they would be coming and had spent the winter getting ready to receive them. They had spent the long rainy winter months knitting and mending their nets, cleaning and repairing their boats, and preparing themselves mentally for going out on that huge, treacherous, dangerous river where death and destruction were always close at hand.

And in other places in Astoria, other men and women were also getting ready for the salmon. In the big board-and-batten or corrugated tin-covered buildings perched above the water all along the waterfront, the cannerymen were stirring — oiling machinery, ordering supplies, and getting their canneries ready to welcome the silvery horde again. The Chinese crews were already on hand, sharpening their butchering knives and preparing their bunkhouses and labeling rooms for the day when the salmon arrived in the river.

There were others preparing for the arrival of the salmon. Local grocerymen ordered supplies and restaurants planned late hours and added help. The Coast Guard drilled for planned disasters and rescues while ferries and ships put on extra hands to keep watch for drifting nets and boats invisible at night.

Then the salmon arrived suddenly and the town sprang to life. The men in their tiny boats went out and caught the passing salmon while the cannery whistles were calling the housewives and students back to work. The boats came in and out, at times loaded with fish and at other times with empty holds. Lights were on at the cannery docks and the college kids sat on the docks, legs dangling over the water, waiting for the seining-ground scows to arrive after a good tide.

At the whistle's shrill summons, the streets suddenly filled with white-clad, heavy-set Finnish and Norwegian housewives going to their cleaning tables at the canneries. The booted Chinese moved stolidly from their bunkhouses to the canneries, carrying aprons and knives. The college kids arrived at the cannery parking lots in loud cars, boisterous and noisy.

The din and the activity went on day and night for most of the spring and summer as the fish passed by the town, and then suddenly it was over and the town was silent again. The boats came in and were tied to the docks. The nets were repaired and dried at the net racks, and the white-clad women went home again to wait for the next call from the canneries. The college kids returned to the campus, richer than when they left and able to pay for another precious year of schooling. The horses, men, and boats left the seining grounds, and the trapmen repaired the damage done by the year's catch and returned home.

This went on in Astoria year after year but then it began to change. The fish still arrived and passed but in smaller and smaller numbers. Some of the canneries closed their doors and many of the fishermen gave up and went to other fishing areas or got out of the business entirely. The housewives had to depend upon other sources for pin money, and most of the Chinese left the town forever.

Today, Astoria is no longer the fishing capital of the world. Indeed, fishing is no longer really much of an industry in the town. The few gillnetters left are mostly part-timers who teach in schools, work in stores, or do other things during the times when the salmon are not passing. The seining grounds are illegal now as are the traps, fishwheels, and purse seiners. The few salmon coming into the river today are counted, weighed, and apportioned out by bearded and environmentally-minded young men from countless government bureaus, determined to save a species of wildlife already gone. The dams killed them off as did the pollution, the drainage ditches, the loss of gravel beds, and periodic over-fishing by a few commercial and sport fishermen.

The busy canneries are gone too. Barbey's was torn down a few years ago and Union Fishermen's Cooperative cannery, which was bought by the Barbey Packing Corp., is being torn down at the present time. Others have burned or vanished during storms along with the bunkhouses, net racks, and the cold storage buildings. Most of the Astoria waterfront today is a long line of rotting slime-covered pilings jutting out from the river bottom, unused by anyone.

To those of us who were there at the height of the greatness of Astoria, the passing of these people and these things is sad and hard to understand. Where did they all go? Where are the men and women who caught and canned the fish? Where are the boats and the barns and the horses? And where are those great buildings which once lined the Astoria waterfront? Gone, all gone.

But we remember them well. We close our eyes and see the red bulk of Union Fish, the snow-white building of Bumble Bee, the gray buildings of Barbey's, and others.

Remember Arthur Anderson's? Remember New England Fish, Van Camp Seafood and Paragon Packing?

We see the boats and the white-clad women and the Chinese and the buildings again in our minds and wish it was all back again the way it was once. But the salmon are gone now and so is the rest, and perhaps it is best. Nothing like it will ever happen again in Astoria.

But wasn't it grand while it lasted?

Chapter 1

HOW IT ALL BEGAN

In the beginning, there was the river winding its way from the Pacific Ocean, through the deep forests of the Coast Range, through the canyons of the Columbia River Gorge, over the falls at Kettle, Bonneville and Celilo, past the rounded prairies of Eastern Oregon and Washington, and on up through other mountains, rapids, and forests until it reached its source in Columbia Lake in British Columbia.

In its 1,150 miles of movement, the river picked up water from other rivers and creeks: from the Kettle and the Kootenai Rivers in Canada, the Snake, Yakima, Wenatchee and Spokane in Washington, and the Deschutes, John Day, Umatilla, and Willamette Rivers in Oregon during its 8,000 feet drop from source to mouth. There were hundreds of others too numerous to mention but they all contributed to the bulk and volume of the mighty river which dominates an immense area of land in the Pacific Northwest.

The river was both a home and a highway for the salmon. They were hatched up in the far reaches of the river and its tributaries, traveled its length on their journey to the sea, and later returned, retracing their way back to the place of their birth, there to renew their cycle of life.

The most prized of these salmon is the Chinook, called King salmon in Puget Sound and Alaska. It is the largest salmon, often weighing in at forty to fifty pounds. The Chinooks enter the river in two runs, one in the spring and then again in a fall run, after spending from two to six years in the sea. A few of these called jack salmon enter the rivers after only one year of maturing and are, of course, much smaller.

The silver salmon, often called coho, is a smaller fish averaging fifteen pounds. Most of the silvers return to the river in the fall after spending two years in the ocean maturing.

The chum or dog salmon returns to spawn in the fall after three to five years in the ocean. They average ten pounds, while the blueback, called sockeye in Puget Sound, average only about six pounds.

The humpback or pink salmon are the smallest of the group, weighing in at only four pounds each and having a unique two year cycle of life.

Lastly, there is the steelhead, basically a trout rather than a salmon, but generally regarded as a salmon. Steelheads average twelve pounds and are the only one of the species able to make the spawning journey more than once.

Of them all, the mighty Chinook salmon was the most plentiful and the most desirable. It was the largest, the most abundant salmon, and its firm, red flesh brought the best prices when canned. Small wonder that most of the growth of the fishing industry grew up centering on this single specimen of the salmon family.

For thousands of years, the salmon runs came and went, virtually unmolested. Natural predators and barriers took their toll but the sheer number of salmon in the Columbia River was undiminished until man arrived and began to harvest the abundant supply of fish. Even then, the small number of Indians, the first of the river dwellers, catching and eating the delicious salmon did not make any appreciable difference in the total number of salmon moving along through the waters of the Columbia River. It has been estimated that 50,000 Native Americans caught and consumed about eighteen million pounds of salmon each year before the arrival of the white men.

With the coming of the traders and settlers, the total number of Indians shrank because of disease, and by the 1840s the total population of both Indians and whites in the Oregon Territory was approximately 20,000, evenly divided between the two races. It was during these years that the salmon population reached its highest point.

The records of the earliest explorers and traders to reach the Columbia River show that the salmon was an important part of the native culture of the area at that time. In their journals, Lewis and Clark noted the various uses of the salmon by the Indians and the ceremonies developed for its use, and were themselves intrigued by the salmon as a source of food.

As more and more traders and others visited the Columbia River and settlements were started, the prolific salmon soon caught the eye of many who wished to capitalize on them. The early explorers, traders, and settlers had, of course, used the delicious salmon for food but no one had thought of profiting from them until Capt. John Dominis, commander of the brig *Owyhee,* came to the Columbia river in 1829. He put up more than fifty casks of salted salmon in rum hogsheads at a site he established near present-day St. Helens, Oregon. He purchased the salmon he used from the Indians and may have been responsible for introducing the diseases which killed off 80% of the Indian population during the next few years. Captain Dominis sold his salted salmon in Massachusetts but gave up the trade after finding out that the government required him to pay a duty on his cargo because it was purchased outside the United States. Other individuals and groups came up with the same idea and salteries, as they were called, sprang up at intervals along the river bank, most of them on the north shore.

The process of salting was so simple that anyone could do it. The salmon were each cut into two long slices lengthwise and then piled carefully inside a large cask. Salt brine strong enough to float a raw egg was then poured over them and allowed to remain there for a measured length of time until a brown scum had formed on top. The brine and scum was poured off and the process repeated several times until finally the last pouring of brine was left in the cask. It was sealed, and the salmon would remain preserved for long periods of time, allowing the casks to be shipped on slow-moving vessels long distances. The greatest difficulty found in using this method was to obtain enough suitable casks during those early days before coopers arrived to set up their trade in the area.

The Hudson's Bay Company established a saltery near Pillar Rock under the management of Kenneth McKay. The products from this saltery were sent over to Astoria across the river from where they were shipped on Hudson's Bay Company vessels to European and Hawaiian markets.

Capt. Nathaniel Wyeth, an American, came to the Columbia River with financial backing and elaborate plans for establishing a trading post and salmon fishery, but his venture failed because he was unable to get enough salmon for processing. Dr. McLoughlin of the Hudson's Bay Company could pay more and did in order to keep Wyeth out of the Oregon Territory.

Local Indians were furnishing all of the salmon being used in the various river salteries at that time but that caused some problems, as they fished at only certain times because of local traditions and taboos. For example, they would not eat salmon until the salmonberries were ripe and would not deliver any salmon to the salteries until the wild currants were ripe.

Despite the difficulties of the industry, others arrived to profit from the plentiful Columbia River salmon. Capt. John Couch arrived in 1840, bought a load of salmon, took it back to the East Coast, and sold it for a good profit. Capt. Couch returned in 1842 and set up his own saltery and trading post at Oregon City. He also established another saltery near Pillar Rock.

It was inevitable that sooner or later, white men would see the profits to be made in catching and selling salmon as well as in preserving them, and would enter that field in competition with the Indians. The white men, however, were not bound by any Indian tribal traditions or taboos and swiftly introduced new methods of fishing, and improved on the ones used by the Indians, thereby greatly increasing the supply of fresh salmon available to those in the business of preserving the salmon and selling the preserved product.

Instead of using seines made of woven spruce roots and cedar bark fibers, they made their seines of strong, light twine. Instead of using manpower and canoes to haul the seines out into the water and then back to the shore again with a load of salmon, they eventually used horses and then power boats to do this same task easier and more efficiently. Instead of building fish traps of bark and limbs, they made strong permanent traps with huge posts and strong rope or wire netting.

The white fishermen were not content to merely fish from the beach sands but were soon going out to the sands in the middle of the river to catch the passing salmon. Instead of a fishing spear, they dragged multiple hooked lines through the water. About the only Indian method of fishing they did not improve upon was the dipnetting at Celilo Falls, and yet even here, they built steel cables on which Indians could move out from the shore and fish from previously-unused islands, thereby increasing their haul.

They ignored all of the Indians signs for the beginning of the fishing season and fished when the salmon were moving up the river, regardless of whether the salmonberries or the wild currants were ripe or not.

It was not long until the bulk of the salmon catches were being brought in by white fishermen, and soon the supply of fresh salmon was more than the salteries could handle. It was obvious to many of the early settlers of the Northwest that the Columbia River held an endless supply of a natural resource which could be exploited easily by the right people. There was money to be made in salmon and soon there appeared men who were willing to take chances, just to get some of that ready money.

During the years from 1835 to 1865, the salmon supply in the Columbia River increased dramatically, mostly because the salmon were not being caught in as great a quantity as they had been before that time. The great majority of the Indians who had once fished the river died of disease during that time, and there were not enough white men living and working in the Northwest to make any appreciable dent in the abundant salmon supply. Unmolested, the salmon thrived and the salmon runs during those years surpassed any seen before or since. The salmon were there in huge numbers and were ready to be harvested by anyone.

Unfortunately, new methods for preserving the caught salmon had not developed as fast as the supply. The salteries continued to pack salmon in barrels and brine but the market for this product was not unlimited. Too much of the salted salmon spoiled on the long voyage around Cape Horn to the eastern United States and to Europe so most of this preserved salmon eventually was shipped to the Hawaiian Islands but that limited market was soon oversupplied and the prices plummeted, forcing many of the once-thriving salteries out of business.

The stage was ready for the next actors to appear and in 1866, four men did arrive on the Columbia River with plans to can salmon. The four: George, William, and Robert Hume, and Andrew Hapgood all had experience canning salmon on the Sacramento River in California but they had become discouraged there because of technical difficulties encountered and also because the ready supply of salmon in that river had rapidly diminished in a very few years. They came to the Columbia River and located a salmon cannery site at Eagle Cliff on the Washington side of the river where they built the first salmon cannery. This site, incidentally, was quite a few miles east of the eventual heart of the salmon fishing industry but in those first few years, the cannery location did not matter too much. The salmon were everywhere and could be caught and processed almost anywhere along the deep channels of the Columbia River.

That first year, Hapgood, Hume & Co. put up a pack of 4,000 cases of one-pound cans and the following year increased their production to 18,000 cases. It was obvious that the salmon canning business on the river was off to a good start and offered boundless opportunities to those willing to enter it.

The Hume success did not go unnoticed. Within a year or so, John West opened a new salmon cannery at Hungry Harbor near Megler, Washington, and F.M. Warren set up his cannery at Cathlamet. In 1870, Ellis & Co. opened a cannery at Point Ellice, while J.C. Megler put up one at Brookfield. By 1873, there were eight canneries located at strategic locations along the Columbia River and ten years later, there were thirty-nine of them, all busily canning salmon.

At the same time, others were improving their methods of catching the salmon so that they could keep up with the sudden demand for fresh salmon. Gillnetting had started in the late 1850s when two Americans used them in the vicinity of Oak Point. At about that same time, Jotham Reed began to build fish traps in this same area, following a design he had seen used on a river in Maine. John Harrington went into partnership with a man named Fitzpatrick and operated a seine on Tenasillihe Island, just downstream from Puget Island. The fish wheel, invented by the Williams brothers, first appeared on the Columbia River at Cascade Locks in about 1878. They were never used much on the lower river because of the lack of suitable locations but were adapted by salmon canneries near the rapids at Celilo and proved very successful there. The Seuferts built their first one three miles east of The Dalles, Oregon, in 1884 and continued to build and buy others until they controlled virtually all of the good fishwheel locations along that stretch of the river.

In 1877, the same John Harrington mentioned above teamed up with Richard Everding and Sylvester Farrell and set up a salmon cannery at Pillar Rock. They put up a pack of 4,000 cases in 1867 and increased that to 15,000 cases in 1870. Their Pillar Rock Packing Co. was successful from the start and stayed in business for many years before being absorbed by the New England Fish Co. in 1930.

Wily Patrick J. McGowan, who came to the Pacific Northwest and purchased 320 acres of land in 1853 near Chinook, Washington, set up a saltery along the flat shoreline there and operated it for many years. He kept an eye on the efforts of Hume and the other early salmon packers, waiting until many of the problems of those first salmon canneries had been ironed out before trying his own hand at canning salmon. Finally, in 1884, he built a cannery which thrived and lasted until 1947, operating long after many of the other canneries had closed. The McGowan Packing Co. eventually transferred its operation to Ilwaco after the Chinook fish traps had been outlawed. McGowan lived to the ripe old age of ninety-five as the patriarch of the early salmon canners of Washington.

It is not to be supposed that this sudden growth of a new industry missed the sharp business eyes of the residents of Oregon on the south side of the Columbia River. The businessmen of Astoria, Oregon, saw the possibilities of canning salmon and set up their own canneries as soon as they could.

Astorians quickly realized that most of the migrating salmon moved eastwards towards the spawning grounds along the channels of the north shore of the river and would always be caught on that side. Astoria, however, had the advantage when it came to canning the salmon. Astoria had a deep water port while the Washington side of the river had none in that area, and the canned salmon could be more easily shipped from Astoria on ocean going vessels. Astoria had a large population from which fishermen and cannery workers could be drawn. It also had financial institutions to solve the industries' money problems, and it had plenty of waterfront property to build cannery buildings on. Looking at these advantages, it is no wonder that soon after Astoria entered the salmon canning industry, it dominated the industry all along the river.

The first cannery to appear in Astoria was Badollet and Co. In 1873, John Badollet, in partnership with Christian Lienenweber, Hiram Brown, John Hobson, and John Adair, established their salmon cannery at Uppertown, in the eastern end of the already ancient city. A few years later, the Scandinavian Cooperative Cannery was built in the same area by a group of Norwegian fishermen and the era of salmon canning in Astoria was off to a running start.

There were others in Astoria who saw a prosperous future in the salmon canning business and acted promptly. Marshall J. Kinney erected a cannery and put up a 50,000 case pack in 1876, his first year in the business. In the following year, J.O. Hanthorne set up one of the largest canneries on the river. In 1874, the Adair brothers, S.D. and John Jr., went into business with A. Booth and erected the A. Booth & Co. salmon cannery.

By 1875, Astoria had become the salmon packing center of the world. In that year, twenty-four ships left for foreign and domestic ports with cargoes of canned salmon. Suddenly, the growth of salmon canneries had made the small town of Astoria into a major shipping point.

The salmon packing industry brought opportunity and wealth to many other Astorians in other lines of work. The influx of fishermen, many of them young and single, created the growth of the boarding house, mainly in the west end of town. At one time, there were nineteen boarding houses lining Taylor Avenue, mostly catering to the Finnish fishermen. The language spoken there was Finnish, and the food was the typical Finnish fare with some new American touches. Paralleling the growth of the boarding houses was the establishment of steam baths in Uniontown, a necessity to the average Finn. Restaurants, clothing stores, and bars sprang up although there is no record of a single brothel in that part of town. That industry was controlled locally by the sinful elements of Astor Street, famous throughout the world as one of the finest red-light districts anywhere. Astor Street was but a short walk from Uniontown so the lack of brothels in that district did not create any great problem for the average young single fisherman.

Uniontown was not the only part of Astoria to grow because of the sudden growth of the Astoria salmon packing business. Uppertown at the east end of the city on the far side of Scow Bay had a similar growth although here the Norwegian and Swedes gathered to live and work. The Chinese cannery workers too, created a need for another ethnic section so a small tight community sprang up near 6th and Bond, just on the outskirts of the city proper. Here, Chinese stores, gambling houses, and all of the other businesses catering to the Chinese worker built an odd community, tight and secret, and yet colorful and at times even glamorous and exciting to the other Caucasian Astorians who were able to catch only occasional glimpses of this Oriental world in their midst.

It was no accident that the canneries and their parallel industries were built away from the main part of Astoria. The men who financed and built the salmon packing plants lived on the hill above Astoria and wanted to keep the fishing industry out of sight. It smelled at times and the many workers imported to keep it going were definitely not the kind of people Astorians were accustomed to associate with so they built their industries on the outskirts, along the waterfronts on the west and east ends of the town. They passed ordinances keeping out certain types of businesses. For example, until the Weinhard-Astoria Hotel was built near the turn of the century, with the condition that it be allowed to operate a bar on the premises, no bars were allowed to operate south of Bond Street. Brothels were certainly kept in one single section of town, out of sight and yet handy to all sections of the town.

Needless to say, many other industries and businesses sprang up to cater to the sudden needs of the fishing and packing industries. Typical of these was John Jackson of Uppertown who set up a sail shop and eventually made most of the sails used by the early-day gillnet boats. He introduced new ideas in sails and also invented the canvas tent designed to fit over the bow of the then-open gillnetter, providing a shelter from the elements for the working fisherman.

Wilson & Fisher, ship chandlers, had a store at the corner of Bond and 7th Streets, and handled oakum, pitch, tar, and other ships provisions as did Foard & Stokes at their new store built in 1891. Adam Van Dusen also had a hardware and ship chandlery and in addition, sold marine insurance.

The Astoria Iron Works on 8th Street and S. Arndt & Ferchen catered to the needs of the new cannery business, specializing in cannery dies and machinery. The Astoria Cooperage provided barrels of all kind while J. Hess sold sails at his sail loft on Bond street. Gilbert & Christiansen did first class blacksmithing on order, while ice for the canneries at first was supplied by W. McCormick who carried ice from Lake Cocolalla and did a roaring business until the canneries opened their own ice plants.

Boat building shops opened their doors in the areas at either end of the town and began turning out all of the various types of boats used by the fishing industry. Machines shops created and repaired machinery for the canneries, clothing stores for the working man opened, and building contractors prospered as did carpenters and other skilled craftsmen needed by the new industry. It is no wonder that the population, wealth, and political power of the town soared during that time.

It was Astoria's finest hour and one that unfortunately lasted only a short time. Within a hundred short years, the Columbia

River fishing industry came and went, leaving Astoria and other communities dependent on the fishing industry struggling to fill the employment and financial gap left by the sudden departure of the salmon fisheries.

Chapter 2

HOW THEY CAUGHT THE SALMON

From time immemorial the Indians living along the Columbia River were the only ones catching the salmon migrating up the river to the spawning grounds far to the north and east. Using methods handed down from generation to generation, these Indians caught as many salmon as they needed for food and for trading purposes.

The Indians used different methods of fishing on different parts of the river, mostly because the different types of topography dictated different methods. What worked on the wide waters of the river near the mouth did not work on those parts of the river where the current ran swift and strong over falls and rocks.

The Chinook and other tribes along the lower reaches of the river used nets made of a twine spun by themselves from spruce root fibres, or from a kind of strong grass brought to the area from the north. Dry cedar pieces of wood were used for floats, and the bottom of the nets was weighted with round beach rocks, laboriously notched to keep them from slipping off the nets. Both the floats and the weights were held in place by cedar strands, woven into place along the top and bottom of the net. These nets or seines were of different lengths ranging from 100 feet up to 600 feet, and were woven into different depths from seven to sixteen feet deep to match the river's bottom and contour.

The fishing began at high tide, just as the waters began to ebb and move out towards the sea. A canoe usually manned by two men would move out along the shoreline where the water ran slower, carrying the net in the back end of the canoe. A third Indian stood on the shore, holding a tow line attached to one end of the seine. At a certain point, the canoe would turn and move swiftly out into the current away from shore while one of the Indians would let out the net behind them as they moved. When all of the seine was in the water, the canoe would then be paddled as fast as possible back to shore, trailing another rope tied to the other end of the seine. As they were doing this, the outgoing current would carry the net and canoe towards the mouth of the river. The man on the shore would follow the progress of the seine, holding tightly to his end of it with his rope.

When the canoe with the tie rope reached shore, the men there and the one holding the tie rope would be joined by others waiting on the shore, and together they would all pull the seine in to shore, hopefully dragging in a big catch of salmon at the same time. As the seine came in, others waded out to meet it, clubbing the salmon on the head to keep them from jumping out of the seine or from swimming under it. When the catch was in, it was divided among the various members of the tribe.

Long spears were used by some Indians in waters clear enough and shallow enough to warrant their use. Migrating salmon tend to group in certain areas, resting and waiting to make the next run over a rapids or falls. At these places, spears could be used to advantage.

Dipnets were used by most of the upriver tribes along such turbulent stretches of rivers as Willamette Falls, Kettle Falls, and especially Celilo Falls, where at times more than 4,000 Indians from various tribes gathered to harvest the salmon moving over the falls.

The dipnet was simply a hoop measuring about four foot across which was attached to a long pole. The net was fixed to the hoop and was designed to close up into a bag when the salmon's weight was in it. When in the swift water, the bag was open at the bottom but when the salmon bumped it, the Indian fisherman would pull it straight up out of the water, snaring the salmon. Most dipnet fishermen built wooden platforms out over the water and fished just above the rushing water with only a rope tied around his waist and the other end looped around a nearby tree or rock to save him if he suddenly toppled into the swift-running rapids below.

Many Indians along the river constructed weirs across some of the narrower streams to catch the migrating salmon. It was a simple fence built of branches woven together which effectively blocked the entire stream. The salmon would come to this and would follow it into another weir where the fish could be easily taken out with spear or dipnet. Needless to say, these weirs had to be rebuilt each year because current and debris coming down the river during the high water season would sweep away these fragile structures with ease.

Once the white men started to fish for Columbia River salmon, the entire picture changed. For one thing, the white man's diseases had killed off approximately 80% of the Indian population by the time the white traders, settlers, and others were ready to enter the fishing business so there was little native competition for them to cope with. Certainly, if the Indian population had remained stable without being decimated, there would have been problems between the white and Indian fishermen but fate intervened and the white men had a virtual open river to use without having to worry about competing with the native fishermen. Celilo and Kettle Falls were exceptions to this for the most part although the fish wheels did compete with Indians later, in many cases driving them away from their traditional fishing spots.

For the next hundred years, there were eight major groups of fishermen operating on the Columbia River at different times, each group competing with the others for a share of the available salmon passing up the river on their way to the spawning grounds. Each group had an advantage over the others in one way or another, but none of them were capable of catching all of the passing salmon by themselves. Conversely, there were neither enough good fishing locations to go around, nor enough salmon to fill all of their needs and wants, so that same hundred years was filled with battles, both physical and legal, for the rights to fish for the Columbia River salmon.

These eight groups were the gillnetters, the trap men, the seiners, the purse seiners, the fishwheelers, the dipnetters, the trollers, and the sportsmen. Perhaps a ninth group should be added to be called the thieves because the history of the fishing industry has been spotted with incidents of people operating outside of the law, taking salmon for their own convenience and profit. Included in this group would be the pitchforkers who took many salmon from shallow waters with pitchforks, using them for food or even for fertilizer, the poachers who fished with nets during closed seasons, and the actual fish thieves who periodically stole fish from traps owned by others. Most of these practices have been curbed in recent years although there have been recent cases involving Indians illegally fishing thus breaking the rules set up for their own benefit.

The most powerful and largest group of fishermen on the Columbia River was the gillnetters, commercial fishermen who used small boats and drifting nets to catch the salmon out on the river. From a small beginning in the 1850s of two men and a gillnet patterned after one used in Maine, the group grew until it reached a total of approximately 2500 individual boats out on the river during some years. This total varied from year to year, depending upon the quantity of fish available, and such other factors as the health of the salmon market, the availability of men, and the river conditions, but in any given year, the gillnetters outnumbered those fishing in other ways and this preponderance of individuals gave the group sporadic power over the other groups. This condition lasted until another group, the sports fishermen, grew larger and eventually had more votes and therefore more power than the gillnetters, a condition which drastically altered fishing regulations on the Columbia River and will continue to do so in the future.

A gillnet is a simple rectangular piece of netting, usually with a mesh measuring 8 inches, just large enough to permit a Chinook salmon to thrust his head into and yet small enough to snare him and keep him there. Later, smaller sizes were used to catch the smaller species of salmon. Originally, the netting was made with cotton twine but was gradually changed as new materials became available. Cedar corks with holes through which the lead line was threaded were placed at intervals along its length to keep it afloat, while lead sinkers were attached to the bottom to keep it down under the water.

One end of the gillnet was fastened to a buoy and the other to the boat. The net, measuring anywhere from 750 feet to 1200 feet, was let out and allowed to drift with the current or tide while the boat remained at its end of the gillnet. When the drift was completed, the boat would move along the gillnet while one of the men pulled the net in, removed any salmon found in the net, and then, after the net was entirely in, would repeat this maneuver as often as possible during that fishing session.

According to records available, Peter Dorcich, an Astoria fisherman, caught the most salmon ever when on July 27, 1904, he made two drifts and singlehandedly caught 4,495 pounds of Chinook salmon. In his first drift, he netted 2,595 pounds, and in the second, he pulled in 1900 pounds.

For a season's catch, Ben Johnson of Astoria is probably the all-time high man with a total catch in 1913 of 46,800 pounds of salmon, according to the *Pacific Fisherman.*

Through the years, methods of gillnet fishing have changed as new improvements have been devised. At first, the gillnetters used a double end boat. It was sailed to the drifting grounds and then a boat puller took over and maneuvered the boat along the net using oars. There have been many photographs made of the "butterfly fleet" showing hundreds of gillnetters sailing out on the river using the unique sail designed for these boats.

After the turn of the century, gillnetters began to use gasoline engines on the boats and within ten years or so, the majority of boats were engine-powered and the glamorous "butterfly" sail had vanished forever.

Gillnetting was a dangerous business and it was a rare year when less than a score of deaths were recorded. The greatest disaster to ever hit the fishing fleet was in May, 1874 when a sudden squall hit the river and the fleet before the fishermen could take any measure to avoid the catastrophe. Boats were scattered with many being driven against the shore or up on a sand bar. First reports placed the number of men lost that day at more than a hundred but later, as the missing men began straggling in, the total was lowered until it officially stood at twenty-six. Even then, some of those listed as dead could have landed safely along the shore and, discouraged, given up the fishing business and gone on to other places without letting anyone know they were safe. Most of them were young single men at that time without local ties or obligations and were free to leave.

In the beginning, the canneries held all the power and did more or less as they pleased. They owned the gillnet boats and the gear and rented them to the men for a price. The fishermen were expected to bring their catch to the home cannery and accept the price offered by the packer. Because most of the fishermen then were young men just over from Scandinavia, they took what was offered without argument. As time went on, however, more and more men owned their own boats and were able to negotiate for better prices and fishing conditions because of their independence. In addition, there were many men fishing in the early day who were only part-timers, men who had farms or small businesses and found that the money made during the fishing season was enough in many cases to carry them through the lean months.

Even so, the salmon canneries set the price of salmon in the early days and the fishermen had to take what was offered. There were times, also, when the canneries had too many fish coming in and had to limit the number of salmon or the amount of pounds they would buy from each fisherman. If he had caught more salmon than the cannery would buy, he had no choice but to dump the extra salmon into the river.

It was inevitable that the fishermen would resent the salmon packers' power and want some say in the matter of price so it was also inevitable that they would form some kind of an organization which would give them more power collectively than they had individually. In the 1880s, the gillnetters organized the Columbia River Fishermen's Protective Union for that purpose. In addition to trying to control prices, the gillnetters also wanted to protect some of their rights including recognized drifting grounds. Because of internal dissension, and unstable fishing conditions, this first organization vanished but was replaced in 1886 by a second Columbia River Fishermen's Protective Union which lasted for ten years.

For the first time, the salmon packers on the river had to face organized opposition to many of their policies and were forced to make concessions on prices paid. The union also fought for lights on some of the islands to lessen their hazard, worked together to remove snags from the bottom of the river, and for the first time began to move against the other forms of fishing such as the traps in Bakers Bay.

The great fishermen's strike of 1896, which lasted for three months and resulted in violence and death, eventually proved the undoing of the CRFPU because, even though they did win concessions from the packers, the strike also made the salmon packers band together for the first time to set standard prices which would be observed by each cannery. The strikers claimed victory by getting 4½ cents a pound for their salmon but by doing so, they lost the eventual battle because the packers began to stick together, holding the line on prices and, during the following twenty years, the price paid went up only about a cent a pound to six cents in 1917.

It was no accident that in 1896, many of the gillnetters went together and formed their own canning organization, the Union Fishermen's Co-Operative Packing Co. and also that three years later in 1899, eight of the major salmon packers on the Columbia River organized themselves into a new salmon packing company, the Columbia River Packer's Assn. Both of these moves were the results of that disastrous strike. The fishermen thought they could do better by organizing their own cannery whereas the packers thought they could also do better by combining their facilities. Both of these moves proved successful although neither eliminated many of the problems of the fishermen and the salmon packers.

The fishermen's union passed out of existence in 1917 but in the following year, the Columbia River Fishermen's League was organized which lasted for a few years but was eventually replaced with a new CRFPU in 1926.

The gillnetters' major competitors before the purse seiners arrived were the trapmen of Chinook, Washington. They competed directly with the gillnetters for the salmon of the lower river which caused an eventual conflict between the

*Workers pull salmon out of a fish trap near Chinook, Washington.
(Photo courtesy Columbia River Maritime Museum)*

two groups and finally, the elimination of the smaller group
through efforts by the larger. It was on this battlefield that
the gillnetters first flexed their collective muscles, both
physical and legal, to get rid of unwanted competition.

After the first trap was installed in Bakers Bay by Oliver
Graham in 1879 and proved a success, other followed in rapid
succession until more than 500 traps filled almost every empty
space in the shallow bay. Most of these were erected and
maintained by residents of Chinook, a small village which
grew and prospered with its new-found fish trap riches, and
which declined just as rapidly after the traps were declared
illegal.

Traps were built here and there along other stretches of
the river where shallow water with a good sandy bottom
allowed the poles of the trap to be driven. Indeed, Henry
Barbey owned one trap at Jim Crow Point, a few miles up
the river on the north side, and used a small crew to operate
it. He later built three traps on Sand Island, but generally,
Bakers Bay was the best single area in which traps were
successful so the trap industry centered around the bay and
the town of Chinook.

The salmon, after entering the river, followed a course

which meandered along the north shore, passing through Bakers Bay on their way eastwards. In the early days, Ilwaco gillnetters had drifted their nets in the bay during favorable tides, but once the traps were built, they created barriers, forcing the gillnetters to move their nets further out on the river. Legally the traps had to be set far enough apart to allow boats to navigate the bay but these channels did not provide sufficient space for a gillnetter's net to drift properly.

In the beginning, the poles for the trap were put in by hand but proved to be so unstable and temporary that this method was soon replaced with one using larger poles put into place by piledrivers. The "lead" line of posts was driven in a straight row leading into a "pot" which had four sides. Both the "lead" and the "pot" had strong four-inch mesh nets which had been dipped into hot tar, both to make it stronger and more durable, and to make it more invisible to the migrating salmon.

Leading away from the pot was a tunnel-like tube of netting set at about the high-water mark. The salmon found this and headed for deep water which, of course, led them into the trap itself, another four-posted affair completely enclosed by more tarred netting. The salmon never thought to swim back the way they came so they remained in the trap, milling around, until they were lifted out by the trap fisherman.

The fishermen used an eighteen foot flat bottomed boat about six feet wide, as completely tarred as were the nets, and would enter the trap by dropping a part of the net and then rehanging it after they were in the trap itself. To get the fish up to the surface where they could be gaffed and lifted out, they simply lifted a part of the bottom net and hung it on a peg set into one of the posts. They would then move along the wall of the trap and lift another corner. They kept this up until the salmon were all on the surface and at that point would begin to harvest their catch. The boat moved from one side of the trap to the other, parts of the net being lifted and hung on wooden pegs attached to the side of the boat as they moved. Scrap fish and undersized salmon would be tossed out of the trap and the mature salmon would be taken aboard until they had a full load at which point they would lower their netting again and leave the trap. If, after they had a boat load, there were still salmon remaining in the trap, they would be left until the next day or the next lift. Trap fishermen often boasted that they wasted no fish by using their method.

The trap fishermen always wore gum boots and oilskins while working. Even so, the tar from the boats and the nets soon covered every exposed inch of skin and they emerged after a day's work in the traps, tarred, black and grimy. It was said along the Columbia River waterfront that residents of Chinook could always be picked out of a crowd by their blackened hands, face, and necks.

Before the salmon season began each year, the entire waterfront at Chinook would be covered with tar dripping from nets and boats, newly dipped into the hot tar vats. Black smoke from the hundreds of boiling tar pots, hung over the entire valley, even blackening the train which moved through the area once a day. Residents of Chinook, however, did not mind the tar smoke or strains in the least. "That black stuff is money," one grimy resident boasted once, and it was true. The tiny village had one of the state's highest per capita income during the trap fishing years.

While most of the traps were owned by individuals, P.J. McGowan & Sons, whose cannery was located nearby, owned and operated traps at Point Ellis, and a few other were owned by various canning companies but most of the fishermen were independents and sold their catch to fish buyers operating out of Chinook.

The first few traps put into the waters of Bakers Bay did not cause too much concern among the early gillnetters because there was still plenty of fish to go around. Later, as time passed and more and more traps appeared in the bay, gillnetters began to grumble about the huge catches made by the trappers, and by the hundreds of poles and nets which dotted Bakers Bay. Even though the traps were set 600 feet apart, they still interfered with the gillnetters fishing methods, so it was inevitable that trouble would break out between the advocates of the two different fishing methods.

In the early 1880s, gillnetters, most of them from Ilwaco,

began making night raids on traps, cutting nets, emptying traps, and doing as much damage as they could. Even though most of the traps soon were guarded by night watchmen, they were generally ineffectual against the gillnetters and the raids continued. During these first few years, several men were killed on both sides, and thousands of dollars worth of traps and nets were destroyed.

The great fishermen's strike of 1896 involved both gillnetters and trapmen, and perhaps it was inevitable that rumors soon spread through both camps that others were selling salmon in spite of the strike. Violence increased to a point where the Washington National Guard was ordered to Sand Island to try and bring order to the chaotic area. Eventually, the Washington National Guard was replaced by federal troops because Sand Island was federally owned, despite Oregon and Washington's claims to the contrary.

Violent acts were committed by both sides and resulted in at least twenty deaths and more than twice that number of injuries, but an uneasy peace was finally achieved after the strike was finally settled by a secret ballot.

The matter was not resolved completely until fish traps were outlawed by the State of Washington in 1934. Because almost all of the successful fish traps were located within the boundaries of Washington, the law effectively eliminated that method of fishing forever.

Chapter 3

SALMON PACKING AT PILLAR ROCK

Who was it that first told Henry Barbey about the Pillar Rock cannery? Was it a salesman coming through Portland who first relayed the information about the non-operating cannery or was it a fisherman down at Ilwaco, perhaps? Maybe Henry Barbey simply learned about it in an overheard conversation at the fish market. In any event, he heard that the old-time Pillar Rock cannery near the mouth of the Columbia river would not be operated during the fall salmon season of 1912. It was simply because the fishing season had just been too good and Everding & Farrell, owners of the Pillar Rock cannery, thought that if they canned too much salmon, they might have a difficult time selling the larger pack.

In 1912, Henry Barbey was a twenty-nine-year-old-single man who was the owner of the Barbey Fish Company of Portland. He had worked for his uncle Edward Chloupek of the Chloupek Fish Co. for a number of years and had eventually bought him out.

Manuel Schnitzer of Portland remembers the Barbey Fish Co. very well. "It was a brick building on Taylor street between 1st and 2nd Streets", he said, "and was built on a twenty-five by one hundred foot lot. My father, Sam Schnitzer, and Henry Barbey were good friends in those days. Even after Henry took his operation to Flavel, they still met. Whenever we stopped at Henry's cannery, he would always give us a case of fish to take along with us. Henry Barbey was a friendly, generous man."

The Barbey Fish Company in Portland dealt primarily in fresh fish, buying and selling wholesale, but in those early days, keeping the fish fresh was always a problem. Refrigera-

*Henry Barbey, president of the Barbey
Fish Co. of Portland.*

*The Barbey Fish Co. building in Portland in 1914. (Photo courtesy
Oregon Historical Society.)*

tion and quick freezes were still in the future and ice was the only means available to insure the freshness of the fish. There is nothing in nature that spoils faster or loses its flavor quicker than fresh fish. As any fisherman knows, the best eating fish is the one caught and immediately cooked and eaten on the spot.

On his many trips to the mouth of the Columbia river during his summer vacations at Seaview, Washington, where his parents had a cottage, Henry had seen the fishing fleets, the buying stations, the seining grounds, and the canneries, and had come to realize that his future in the fish business lay in the packing end. Only fish processed in this manner could be brought to market in as good a condition as when it was caught.

Now it was the summer of 1912 and Everding & Farrell's Pillar Rock Packing Co. was not going to put up a fall pack. The season would end, the summer pack would be sold, and the cannery would lay idle until the following spring. There was a full crew there, ready to work through the fall if the cannery remained open. The machinery was all in place, fully operational, and certainly, the fall run of salmon would be entering the river as usual, passing Pillar Rock on its way up to the spawning grounds hundreds of miles away.

Henry Barbey heard about Everding & Farrell's decision to close the cannery after the spring run ended and he acted. He knew that this was the opportunity he had been waiting for — the chance to get into the salmon packing business without a big outlay of cash.

Certainly there would be expenses but Henry Barbey already had connections in the business world. He coolly negotiated a loan with the United States National Bank in Portland. R.W. Schmeer, the senior loan officer there, gave him the necessary line of credit based on his business reputation because Henry Barbey had little collateral. He was gambling that the fall run would be a good one and that he would be able to sell his pack without any trouble. It was a gamble but Henry was a natural-born gambler who didn't mind staking his all on his own ability. He gambled but it was a calculated gamble and so in his mind, no gamble at all.

*Henry Barbey (left) and friend
Henry Wagner at a family picnic.*

The Pillar Rock Packing Company was named for a peculiar rock formation which juts out from the waters of the Columbia River about twenty miles from its mouth. This odd rock is near the north shore with a navigable channel running between it and the shore, and was first sighted and named by Lt. William Broughton on Oct. 25, 1792 on his river-exploring expedition for Capt. George Vancouver. Meriwether Lewis and William Clark also noticed the rock on Nov. 8, 1805 when they described it as "a rock at the distance of a mile in the river, about twenty feet in diameter and fifty in height."

On the shore north of Pillar Rock was the location of the old Hudson's Bay saltery, an early-day fish salting operation. This was the spot which Sylvester Farrell and Henry Everding chose as the site for their new salmon cannery in 1878. In company with John Harrington, they built the packing plant and put up a pack in that first year which they shipped out on the sailing ship *City of Chester*. By 1881, the new Pillar Rock Packing Company was putting up 15,000 cases with a value of approximately $67,500. This was the time of the hey-day of the salmon packing industry on the Columbia River and Everding & Farrell was getting its share of the profits.

But by 1912, things had changed. Sylvester Farrell died in 1909, and in 1910, John Harrington left the area and moved to England where he spent the remaining years of his life. The owners of Everding & Farrell were by this time more interested in logging, and their Deep River Logging Co. was occupying more and more of their time. A long-time employee named Billy Starr was put in charge of the packing plant and he kept it running as a profitable part of the Everding & Farrell business enterprises. Certainly, the Pillar Rock Packing Co. was a first-class salmon packing operation and, if it could be leased for even one season, Henry Barbey was ready to lease it.

Henry arrived at the packing plant to find a full crew waiting for him. As soon as the season opened, the plant began operations and by the end of that first season, Barbey found that he had a good pack ready to be sold, but no ready buyers waiting to buy.

Henry Barbey did not hesitate. If the buyers did not come to him, he would go to the buyers. He took samples of his first pack with him on a train to New York where the canned-salmon buyers at the different wholesale grocers were located and called on them with a new idea. To prove the good quality of his pack, he invited the buyers to open and taste the canned salmon. Sig Seaman, one of the owners of Seaman Bros. in New York City, was so impressed by the young man from Oregon and by his forthright method of selling his pack that he bought the entire fall pack for his "White Rose" label. This was the beginning of a long and happy relationship between the Barbey Packing Co. and Seaman Bros. Each year, Sig Seaman was on hand to buy as much salmon from Barbey as his "White Rose" label could use.

Before he left for New York, Henry had converted his

warehouse filled with canned salmon into a bonded warehouse in which a receipt for the warehouse was taken to a bank and money was loaned on this stored salmon. To release the salmon, it was necessary to pay back the money borrowed from the bank plus interest. The bank was protected by sending representatives to the different warehouses unannounced to check to see that the bonded salmon was actually there. It was a method which worked because everyone concerned had faith in the system and adhered rigidly to the rules set down.

Within a few years, however, Henry Barbey had made enough money to finance his own salmon pack each year and no longer had to use this method of financing. He was proud of his relationship with his bank which would give him a line of credit to finance his yearly pack on his signature alone with no collateral requested. Very few of his competitors could boast of having this privilege.

In addition to leasing the Everding & Farrell plant each year, he also bought fresh fish on the coast and along the river and had it shipped to Portland where he sold it wholesale to the various markets in that inland city.

During that first year in the salmon packing business, Henry Barbey had not put all of his eggs into just one basket. He also branched out into the fish buying business down near the mouth of the Columbia River, selling the fresh fish to a variety of buyers. One of these, J. Lindenberger, bought $1800 worth of steelhead from Barbey to be processed for the German market overseas. In addition to this, he was also shipping fresh salmon to the Chloupek Fish Co. of Seattle as well as to the Barbey Fish Co. of Portland.

Barbey kept his main office in Portland and put a man named Jack Elia in charge of his downriver fish buying business. Jack turned into a long-time employee as well as a personal friend of Henry Barbey. The two went duck hunting together and there is a tale about a white barn owl which Jack shot and had stuffed as a gift for his employer. Henry Barbey put this owl on the company safe where it remained for more than sixty years. It was considered a wise old owl and brought good luck to the company as long as

A Barbey fish buying scow tied up for winter at the Barbey moorage on the John Day river, just east of Astoria. The Mayday *is also moored just in front of the scow.*

it guarded the old company safe. After Graham Barbey, Henry's son, sold the company in 1974, one of the new owners took the old owl to a taxidermist to be cleaned. By this time this particular species of owl had been named an endangered species and irate environmentalists wanted to have the new owner prosecuted for shooting an owl protected by environmental laws.

Gradually, Henry Barbey began to build an empire at the mouth of the Columbia River. He started small with his leasing of the Pillar Rock Packing Co., but then branched out with fish buying stations at Ilwaco, Chinook, and Hammond. He bought several small launches which went out to the fisherman and bought their catches for cash on the barrelhead. One of these, the *Rambler,* ran out of Hammond under the command of Capt. R.M. Voeth.

In 1912, Henry Barbey had taken a big step into an unknown future. He was only twenty-nine years old that year and already had his own business in Portland and was branching out on a large scale in the Lower Columbia area. What made him do it? Why was he not content, as so many other men would have been, in staying in Portland and operating his fish company there without taking the obvious risks entailed in expanding his small fish business into an unknown area and a new, unfamiliar industry.

Katherine Barbey, widow of Henry's brother Daniel, put it best in a 1986 interview when she said, "Henry was bright." She thought for a moment and then went on. "All of the Barbeys are bright. They are bright and they are ambitious to do the best they can. Second best is never enough. Dan was that way too which was why he ended up an admiral in the navy. He was not content with less and neither was Henry. It was something inside of them that made them want to succeed, not for fame or anything like that but simply for their own satisfaction. Each of them had to prove it to himself. It was in their blood."

It was indeed. The Barbey bloodlines can be traced back to 1573 when the Barbey family was living in Normandy, France. They were Huguenots, a name given to French Protestants, and, because of the persecution of Huguenots in France at that time, the Barbey family fled to Germany to take up a new life there.

Jacob Frederick Barbey, Henry's grandfather, was born March 14, 1827, in Winden, Germany, and emigrated to the United States where he settled in Buffalo, New York. He married and had three boys but his first wife died at an early age. Jacob remarried and then found that the new stepmother did not want the responsibility of raising three active boys so they were given to other families to raise.

John Barbey, Henry's father, was given to a family named Fehrs who apprenticed the boy to a local locksmith. After completing his apprenticeship, John ran away and headed

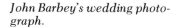

John Barbey's wedding photo-
graph.

Julia Barbey's wedding photo-
graph.

west, eventually ending up in Portland, Oregon. Here, he
went into business for himself as a locksmith and sewing
machine agent.

In 1879, John Barbey was advertising himself in the local
newspapers as an agent for all kinds of sewing machines and
as a sewing machine repairman. Locks, keys, bell hangings,
and fine machinery were also made to order by the talented
newcomer. Frances Barbey, John's daughter, many years later
described her father as a combination locksmith and safe
expert. "He opened safes that people couldn't open," she said,
"and he was a skilled mechanic."

John Barbey first opened this business at 32 Yamhill Street
between First and Second Streets in Portland in 1877. He
prospered and soon needed help so he wrote to his brother
Jacob, still working in the East, to come out west and join
him as a business partner.

On Feb. 2, 1881, John Barbey married Julia Chloupek, a
daughter of Wencel and Frances Chloupek. Julia's brother
Edward was the proprietor of the Chloupek Fish Co. of
Portland.

During the next two decades, six children were born to the Barbeys: Blanche Rose, born in 1881; Henry J., born in 1883; Caroline Helen, born in 1888; Daniel Edward, born in 1889; Hazel Marie, born in 1897; and Frances Grace, born in 1902.

During these years, John Barbey prospered in Portland. In addition to his business, he dabbled in real estate, buying and selling property in the growing city. He bought a house on Sixth and Sherman Streets and later bought the two houses next door. Later, he purchased a vacant lot at Tenth and Hall and built an apartment building there which he named the Hermina Apts. This location is now a part of the Portland State College campus. Still later, Barbey moved his family to Irvington at 24th and Knott Streets.

Barbey prospered and was eventually able to buy a summer cottage at Seaview, Washington, because he wanted to get his children out of the city during the summer months. Each year, the Barbey family traveled down the Columbia River on the steamboats *T.J. Potter* or *Hasselo* to Ilwaco, Washington, and then would travel north to Seaview on the Clamshell Railroad, as the local people called the I.R. & N. Co. narrow gauge railroad which ran sporadically up and down the Long Beach Peninsula at that time.

Once he had his family installed in their Seaview cottage, John Barbey would return to Portland, returning to Seaview each week on the "Daddy Special", a steamboat which made the trip each Friday evening from Portland carrying commuters to the beach for a weekend with their families.

Henry Barbey learned to swim at the cottage on the beach at Seaview. He became an excellent swimmer and frequently swam far out to sea, beyond the breakers. Once, he was caught out there by an undertow and spent the next three hours in the icy ocean trying to get back to shore. He was an exceptionally strong swimmer but after that experience, he began carefully following the rules of ocean bathing and always tried to have someone with him during his ocean dips.

Henry and his brothers and sisters attended Portland schools. Henry went to Lincoln High School and, when that school became over-crowded in the early 1900s, volunteered

Henry Barbey trying his fishing luck in 1903.

The Barbey family. John and Julia Barbey with children (top row)
Blanche, Henry and Caroline. (Front row) Hazel, Frances and Dan.

Henry Barbey, a high school graduate from Lincoln High School at Portland.

Henry and Daniel Barbey, ages nine and two.

to attend a new school built farther away to relieve the congestion at the old school. To do this, he had to walk a few extra miles each day, a fact he used many years later when he jokingly chided his own son Graham for complaining about having to walk a mile to his Seaside school.

When the new Lincoln High School was built in Portland in the 1950s, an invitation to some of the old school's distinguished graduates went out, inviting them to attend the dedication of the new school. Unfortunately, Henry Barbey's invitation included the information that he was to sit on the speakers' platform which had a bathroom handy. Henry refused to attend the ceremony, saying angrily that if they thought he was so old that he might have kidney problems, they were badly mistaken.

Henry Barbey never worried about his health and never had a full physical examination until he was over fifty. His advice to anyone who had medical problems was this: "If it is on the outside, apply zinc ointment liberally to the place. If it is on the inside, pour bourbon on it."

Henry Barbey in 1908.

Henry and his brother Dan were very close, even though Henry was six years older. He protected and advised Dan, and Dan admired his older brother tremendously. He told his wife Katherine many years later, "Of all the men I ever met, Henry was the best." That was a high compliment coming from a man who had met and talked with many of the world's leaders during his many years serving his country as a career officer in the United States Navy.

After graduating from high school in 1900, Henry, rather than going on to college, decided to work for his Uncle Edward at his Chloupek Fish Co. Edward was childless and wanted a member of the family to come in, learn the fish business, and keep the company going. Henry went to work there and, with his usual determination, studied and worked hard, and soon became the manager, a post he held until he went into the fish business on his own.

During these years, Henry still lived with the family, helping to keep the other children in line. After Dan graduated from high school, Henry encouraged him to take the competitive examination for Annapolis. Dan was not particularly interested in a career in the U.S. Navy but he did like the idea of getting a free college education so he studied hard and won the appointment for the Naval Academy from Senator Johnathan Bourne.

Mrs. Katherine Barbey, many years later, told about his experiences getting into the Academy.

"In those days, people had to travel to the east coast by train which was a four day journey. By the time he arrived, Dan was in a highly nervous state and fainted during the physical examination. The doctor examining him said that he had a very bad heart and turned him down as physically unacceptable. Dan was lying on the floor in a faint and, as he was coming to, heard the doctor say that he might not last long.

"Dan was frightened and that night wrote a letter to his brother Henry telling him that he could have his watch, the only thing of value he owned, if he died before he could get back to Portland.

"Then, his good common sense took command. He looked up a relative who sent him to a doctor he knew in Washington, D.C. Dan went there and found that the doctor was out. His secretary, however, was so impressed by Dan's determination that she called the doctor back from his holiday to examine Dan. The doctor found nothing wrong and told him to go back and tell them that if they didn't pass him, he would personally go and see the Surgeon General to complain about Dan's situation."

Dan did go back, passed the physical examination, graduated from Annapolis, and went on to achieve lasting fame as Uncle Dan, the Amphibious Man in World War II. He was in charge of eighty-three of the U.S. Navy's amphibious landings and developed many of the techniques used for those landings. He won the Navy Cross as well as

Midshipman Daniel Barbey at Annapolis.

many foreign decorations and retired as one of the foremost U.S. naval heroes of that war.

In the *Lucky Bag*, the Annapolis yearbook, he was called Handsome Dan but the other members of the family always thought that Henry was the handsome one, according to Frances Barbey.

All during these years, the two boys encouraged their sisters to get an education and to do the best that they could. Their sister Frances, who taught school at Catlin School in Portland, later said, "Henry and Dan helped me through Reed College even though I had to work in the dining room there to help out. They both bossed me and I had to be awfully good when they were around."

Even though there was a great disparity in the ages of the various Barbey children, it was a close-knit family, living together in harmony. Henry, the eldest boy, was absent more and more as he prospered in his business ventures, and when he moved into the Lower Columbia fishing industry, he was gone most of the time, but still managed to get back home frequently to visit his family. In his heart, Henry Barbey valued family ties as much as he did success and it showed in the affection the younger Barbey children demonstrated as they talked about him many years later.

Chapter 4

LIFE AT FLAVEL

The Hill Terminals at Flavel, Oregon, were deserted in 1917 and the great docks stood empty. Only a few years before, the place had been a bustling transportation center with two great steamships — the *Great Northern* and the *Northern Pacific* — docking there before making the return trip to San Francisco. Trains came in regularly bringing passengers and freight from Portland and then returning loaded several times each week.

Across the street from the Hill Terminals stood the Flavel Hotel, once called one of the finest on the Pacific Coast but now demoted to a mere rooming house for wartime shipyard workers from Astoria across Youngs Bay.

The beginning of World War I had caused a drastic decline in the fortunes of the once-booming town of Flavel. The United States government had cast covetous eyes on those two mighty steamships and had requisitioned them for wartime uses. The *Great Northern* and the *Northern Pacific* departed for the war and without them, Flavel in a matter of a year or so was virtually deserted.

The two ships had left, but the docks and loading facilities as well as the storage buildings were still there, deserted but ready to be used if a use could be found for them. The Spokane, Portland & Seattle Railway, popularly known as the S.P. & S., owned the Hill Terminals and had recently granted permission to the officials of Clatsop County to use the unoccupied dock and buildings temporarily for the storage of building materials. However, railway officials were looking for a permanent lessee and were ready to cancel the agreement with the county if a legitimate firm would take out a five-year lease on the property.

The Flavel Hotel.

Henry Barbey had a use for the Hill Terminals. He had been waiting for years for an opportunity such as this. As soon as he heard of the availability of the terminals, he traveled down the river to Flavel to see if the former transportation facilities could be used for a salmon cannery.

The Hill Terminals had been opened in June, 1914, and hailed as the beginning of a greater Astoria and the opening of a new era of progress and development. The pier rested on 2,000 piles and the builders had boasted of using 1.3 million feet of lumber in the construction of the Terminals. The depot itself provided 45,000 square feet of storage or a capacity of 12,500 tons. The docks had a 600 foot frontage on the water. There were four miles of side tracks built to service the facility. A huge freight shed as well as the depot was under roof in a setup ideal for a salmon cannery. There were also two oil tanks as well as a huge water tank. Just about everything necessary to operate a salmon cannery was in place. All that was needed was canning machinery and other basic necessities for canning salmon.

Henry Barbey inspected every inch of the Hill Terminals and liked what he saw. He knew that the long docks fronting on deep water and out of the main river current would be perfect for the docking and unloading of purse seiners, gillnetters, and his receiving scows. The big covered buildings had plenty of room in them for the canning machinery, work and storage areas, and for ice rooms, labeling rooms, and office areas.

In the early part of February 1918, the *Astorian-Budget* announced that the Barbey Fish Co. of Portland had leased the Hill Terminals at Flavel and would convert the warehouse into a salmon packing plant to be ready for operation on May 1, 1918. Henry Barbey had made his move and from that time on would have to be considered one of the major salmon packers on the Columbia River.

Henry Barbey filed an assumed business name in July 1919, changing the name of his company from the Barbey Fish Co. of Portland to the Barbey Packing Co. of Flavel.

In the spring of 1917, Henry Barbey was thirty-three years old and still a bachelor. The constant traveling between Portland and the mouth of the Columbia River, and the time-consuming schedule of buying and transporting salmon kept him on the move and left little time for a social life. Even at that time, his work was his life and almost every waking moment of the day was used to further his growing business.

Sometime during those early days of 1917, however, he met a pretty girl named Ethel Graham who was visiting her aunt, Mrs. Alice Thompson of Portland. She had come out west from Clarksville, Iowa, which is located near West Branch, Iowa, the birthplace of Herbert Hoover, and was a first cousin of Lou Henry Hoover, the future president's wife. With his usual single-minded drive, Henry pushed his suit and they were married in Portland on March 21, 1917.

Eleven months later, in February 1918, he leased the Hill Terminals at Flavel, Oregon for the purpose of running his own salmon canning operations. This business move meant that he would no longer be traveling between Portland and the mouth of the Columbia River as often as he had in the past and it was obvious to him that he had to set up a home for his new wife at or near his cannery.

Ethel Graham before her marriage to Henry Barbey.

Henry Barbey and Ethel Graham, later to become Mrs. Barbey, 1917.

Ethel Graham in Portland in 1917.

Across the street from the new Barbey Packing Co. at Flavel was the Flavel Hotel, a magnificent wooden structure. However by 1917 it had fallen on hard times and was serving as a kind of dormitory or rooming house for shipyard workers employed at the Rogers' shipyards, located at Pier 2 of the Port of Astoria. Wartime housing in Astoria had become so hard to find that the shipyard had leased the entire hotel and rented the rooms to its workers at low rates. When the war ended, the shipyard closed and the workers departed for other places leaving the old hotel standing idle once more.

It had once been a beautiful structure, three-storied with a 160 foot north wing and a 120 foot east wing. Built in 1896 by the Flavel Hotel Company, it had been planned as the nucleus of a great city which was to rise on what had once been known as Tansy Point. The promoters of the hotel development had dreamed of railroad lines using the town of Flavel as a terminus, and the steamship lines using it as a major docking facility. The company had spared no expense in the construction of the hotel and the grounds and had even built another building nearby which housed a pool hall, a saloon, and a bowling alley. The grounds included tennis courts, other houses, and a riding academy.

Things had not worked out for the developers and the hotel was sold in 1906 and again in 1914. Better days came then for the town of Flavel when the Hill Terminals were built. The Flavel Hotel boomed and prospered for a few years but then the steamships left taking the hotel's business with them. The town of Flavel declined again and with it the hotel.

During the first year of their marriage, Henry and Ethel Barbey lived in Portland while Henry traveled back and forth between Flavel and Portland. It was soon obvious that the young couple would have to find a place to live near the Flavel cannery. Housing during the war was hard to find in the Lower Columbia area but following the armistice in 1918, the Rogers' shipyard workers moved out of the Flavel Hotel and it was vacant once more.

The vacant hotel was the answer to Henry Barbey's problem. He leased the entire building and moved his wife into a suite on the first floor. Other employees of the cannery

Henry Barbey in front of the Flavel
Hotel in 1919.

were given rooms and apartments in other parts of the
building, but even then a large part of the hotel remained
vacant. At about the same time, Henry Barbey built
bunkhouses near the cannery for his Chinese crew. About
twenty-five workers, the Chinese foreman, and the cook lived
in these, using parts of the grounds for their vegetable gardens.
This housing arrangement made it easier for Barbey and for
his workers to operate the cannery without traveling long
distances to work.

Henry and Ethel Barbey's only child, Graham, who was
born in 1919, recalled living in the big hotel. "It had large
brass chandeliers with white glass fluted shades. It was very
large and the hardwood floors were very handsome."

Undoubtedly, the small boy had an interesting time, exploring all of the nooks and crannies of the old hotel and playing outside on the big lawn.

The Barbeys lived in one of the suites facing the cannery. There were many of these located along the front of the building. Each consisted of a living room, kitchen, and two bedrooms and opened up into the main hall which ran the length of the hotel. On the south wing of the hotel was a huge dining room, and on the east end was a circular lobby. From this lobby, a circular staircase wound its way up to the third floor. The beauty of the old hotel was still present at that time and it was sad to see the huge building virtually unoccupied and unused.

Because the hotel was located far from any shopping facilities, Henry bought his wife a new Packard Twin Six to use for going into Warrenton for groceries and to see friends. Even though the roads in those days were primitive, Mrs. Barbey enjoyed using that car and soon was able to drive all the way to Seaside by herself.

The Packard was involved in one incident which illustrates Henry Barbey's sense of humor, even in the face of possible disaster. A cousin, Mrs. Imre Clausen had come down from Seattle to visit Ethel and Henry. She had a daughter named Betty who was about the same age as Graham Barbey so the two children were able to play together during the visit. One day, the two ladies decided to drive to Seaside in the Packard. The mothers put the two children in the back seat and began driving down the highway but soon came to a place where repairs were being made on it. Traffic was being diverted from the highway to Columbia Beach south of Warrenton. From there, the cars could move along the beach south to Gearhart where they turned back onto the highway.

Unfortunately, the tide was high at that time and the big Packard was caught by the incoming ocean. Ethel Barbey stayed with the car and the children, while Mrs. Clausen walked to Gearhart about five miles south to get help. At that time a black man named Bill Badger lived there who, with his wife, operated a chicken dinner restaurant in their Gearhart home. Mrs. Clausen hired Badger to bring his team

*Ethel Barbey driving the Packard
Twin Six.*

of mules up the beach to pull the Packard out of the water.
First, she called Henry Barbey at the Flavel cannery to tell
him what had happened.

Completely unruffled, Henry infuriated Mrs. Clausen by
telling her to tie the Packard to a log and wait for the tide
to go out. He knew there was nothing he could do about
the stranded automobile, and therefore refused to worry about
it. Obviously he enjoyed his joke but Mrs. Clausen did not.
She and Bill Badger drove up the beach, pulled the big car
out of the surf, and the party resumed their journey to Seaside.
Henry's casual advice to Mrs. Clausen became a family joke
and was brought up each time she visited the Barbey family.

The Packard Twin Six was the catalyst which caused the

Graham Barbey, age 3 at Warrenton, Oregon.

Barbey family to move out of the Flavel Hotel and into a small house at Warrenton. Henry Barbey's parents had come down to Flavel to visit the young couple and had borrowed the Packard to return to Portland because their own car had broken down. Unfortunately, the Packard did not get back to Flavel for some time and this caused Ethel Barbey to become isolated in the almost-deserted town of Flavel. This did not please her very much and she told Henry that she could not stand living in a mostly-vacant hotel with a small child and no transportation. Finally, he moved his family to Warrenton and into a rented house there.

Graham said in later years, "I don't know whether houses in Warrenton were scarce or whether my father felt poor at that time but I do know that it was a mighty small house. I don't know how long we lived there but I can recall my mother hauling buckets of rich soil from a creek bed about two blocks away to make a beautiful flower garden in the yard of that house."

Henry Barbey always loved big heavy cars and he owned two Packards at this time. The house in Warrenton had no garage so he kept the two Packards at the local automobile repair shop which was known as Knight's Garage. About this time, he wanted to sell one of the Packards and buy a Pierce-Arrow sedan for Ethel Barbey so he had the owner of the Warrenton garage take out a dealership and Henry got his new car wholesale. It had a blue body and tan fenders, and also boasted of having the first automobile radio ever sold in Portland. In those days, radio signals were weak and all the radio would get in Warrenton was static, as the nearest radio station was in Portland.

When their son Graham was six years old, they decided to move to Seaside because Henry felt the schools there were better than they were in Warrenton. He rented a house on the Prom and Avenue I for the family and registered Graham in the local grade school. This move, however, meant that he had to commute back and forth to work each day for a distance of about fifteen miles. He had traded his Packard in on a new Stutz Bearcat, one of the sportiest automobiles of the 1920s. It was a noisy car, however, and his family could hear him coming three blocks away each evening when he returned to Seaside from his cannery at Flavel.

During the next few years, the Barbey family developed a living routine which never varied too much from year to year. During the spring and summer months, they lived at Seaside and Henry commuted to the Flavel cannery each day. After the salmon canning season was over and the pack sold, he would close the cannery or else leave it in charge of his foreman. Henry would then take an apartment for November, December, and part of January at the Sovereign Hotel on Broadway in Portland, or at the Ambassador Apartments on Sixth. In February, March and parts of April, he would take the family to Los Angeles for the winter months.

Ethel Barbey in 1923 with her new Paige automobile. Photo was taken in Portland's Washington Park.

He usually rented a cottage there on the grounds of the Chapman Park Hotel on Wilshire Boulevard across from the Ambassador Hotel, famous for the Coconut Grove. Occasionally he rented a house on the Wilshire Country Club golf course on Rossmore street. For several years, he leased half a floor at a large apartment house on Rossmore, while the other half was leased by Mae West, the famous movie star. Graham Barbey recalled that her cook was apparently great on cooking fish and would leave the apartment door open so that the entire floor reeked of fish, an odor "my father really did not appreciate during the winter months." He added, "My parents never really became great friends with Miss West."

The house on the grounds of the Wilshire Country Club was leased from Blanche Bagnall whose husband first electrified Borneo. Bagnall was an electrical engineer and the king of Borneo was so pleased with the electrical system he designed, with its fans to combat the heat as well as lighting, that he opened up a big trunk and gave Bagnall a quantity of uncut diamonds and rubies which he later took to Holland to have cut and mounted. That one venture made him very wealthy. The Bagnalls had another home on the Irvine Ranch which they used when the Barbeys leased their home in Los Angeles.

The Depression did not really hurt Henry Barbey because no matter how bad the times were, people still had to eat. The price of canned salmon declined, but so did labor and other costs at the cannery. It all worked out so that the Barbey family was in comfortable circumstances during those grim years of the Depression.

Living in California during those winter months was peaceful and gave Henry a chance to relax from the hectic pace of the salmon canning business. He and his wife played bridge a great deal with friends but he was a cautious and deliberate player who took his time about which cards to play. He would stare at his hand and then say, "I think I'm going to play this card," and slowly pick it out of his hand. This slow pace exasperated Ethel who often said, "Hurry up, Henry, or I'll get a book to read while you are making up your mind."

On Saturdays, Henry often went to the horse races at Pasadena where he would place small bets on the races. Friends say that he was an absolute genius at picking winners. He was a naturally lucky man but he also studied the records of the horses in each race and made bets based on his estimate of the various horses' ability and speed.

Ethel Barbey, on the other hand, liked to bet on hunches. One day, there was a horse named Hasten Henry running and she thought it would be a sure thing to bet on because she was always after Henry to hurry up to get somewhere. She bet on Hasten Henry to win but the horse stumbled at the starting gate and came in dead last. Henry laughed and said, "See, I told you not to bet on that nag."

The Barbeys gradually built up a circle of friends in Los Angeles. Among these was Judith Scott Walter, daughter of Harvey Scott of the *Oregonian,* whose second husband was Bill Walter, then managing editor of the *Saturday Evening*

Post. Her dinner table was enjoyed by civic and business leaders of the world, as well as leading politicians visiting the Los Angeles area. Although she lived in the movie capital, she never invited Hollywood movie stars because she thought that they were immoral.

Chris Sebastian, owner of the Sebastian-Stewart Fish Co. of Seattle, often joined Henry Barbey at the race track. He owned a race horse named Galadamian and he and Henry made money each time the horse ran. Sebastian was offered one hundred thousand dollars for the horse and turned down the offer. Galadamian was soon after kicked by another horse during a race at Santa Anita and was never able to run again.

It was a good life and the rest and relaxation he got in Los Angeles was comforting, but Henry Barbey would be champing at the bit by the beginning of April and would be anxious to get back to his cannery and once more dive into the competitive and yet uncertain life of the salmon packer. It was his life and he would not have been happy doing anything else. Southern California was fine but to Henry Barbey, there was no place like the area around the mouth of the Columbia River.

Chapter 5

THE FIRST SALMON PACKING SEASON AT FLAVEL

There were many things to be done before Henry Barbey's new Flavel salmon cannery could be operated and time was short. The lease with the S.P. & S., was signed in February 1919, and the fishing season opened on May 1st which meant that in the short period of two month's time, Henry Barbey would have to set up his entire salmon cannery, hire a crew, buy the necessary supplies, and have it all ready to go by the end of April. It was a tight schedule which would have overwhelmed a lesser man but Barbey was a man of action and once his mind was made up to do something, he allowed nothing to stand in his way.

Luckily, he already had a nucleus of experienced cannery employees to take over some of the responsibilities of setting up the canning operation. Jack Elia, who had been in charge of his fish-buying station at Hammond for a number of years and who had been designated local manager of the new cannery during the negotiations for the Hill Terminal lease, was invaluable for handling many of the local problems encountered by the new operation. He had lived at Hammond and knew the people there and at Warrenton and Flavel so he was able to hire the needed carpenters, plumbers, and electricians, and supervised the many alterations needed in the big terminal building to convert it from a warehouse into an operating canning facility. He also helped recruit local girls for work on the packing lines.

Jue Bue Wong, who was familiarly known as Buey, had also been with Henry Barbey for a number of years and came down to Flavel from Portland to act as the foreman of the

Chinese crew which would do all of the salmon butchering and labeling. He helped a Chinese labor contractor round up a crew of twenty-four skilled butchers and slimers and then got them settled in a new bunkhouse which had been hastily erected near the new cannery. It was convenient to the cannery and yet boasted enough space for the Chinese crew to have its own vegetable garden, a necessary part of a Chinese cannery worker's life.

In addition to these men, Barbey already had a full staff of fish buyers who manned his receiving stations scattered at strategic locations all up and down the river, and these were served by Capt. R.M. Voeth, another long-time Barbey employee, who maintained daily contact during the fishing season with the various buyers. Using the launch *Rambler,* he delivered cash to the buyers each day, and picked up the fresh salmon purchased at each fish station, transporting the salmon to the Flavel cannery dock as quickly as possible.

Many sudden problems came up during those two months which had to be solved, sometimes in an odd but inventive manner. One of these was the unexpected problem of getting a large supply of dry wood to be used for firing the boilers which ran day and night during the canning season. Ordinarily, the canneries which used wood for the boilers, contracted each year for the next season's supply. The wood was delivered, stacked, and allowed to dry and weather until the following canning season when it would be used and a new future supply ordered.

Henry Barbey, however, leased the Terminals in February, obviously too late in the year to buy an adequate supply of firewood. There was plenty of wood for sale in the area but it was all green and wet at this time of the year. It was a problem but Henry Barbey solved it in an unusual way.

During World War I, three shipyards had operated in the Astoria area, all with contracts to build wooden ships for use by the United States government in transporting freight and men to the European war zone. Wilson Brothers built them at its yard at Smith Point, Rogers shipyard was at the

The Barbey Packing Co. at Flavel as seen from the Flavel Hotel.

Port of Astoria and McEachern had a shipyard in Williamsport on Young Bay. When the Armistice was signed, the government had no use for these wooden ships and cancelled all contracts, even though many of the hulls still perched unfinished on the now-deserted shipyard ways. A few of them were completed and used while at least one of them was towed across the river, beached and abandoned. It can still be seen there today about a mile east of the Washington entrance to the Astoria Bridge, although during the past seventy years, trees and brush have grown on the rotting hull, turning it into a unique man-made island.

Henry Barbey remembered these wooden hulls and went over to Astoria to look at them. He found one, a massive 300-foot-long wooden skeleton which had been weathering on the ways for more than two years, unneeded and unwanted by anyone. He quickly bought the wreck for a pittance, had it towed over to Flavel and beached it near the new Barbey cannery. He ordered his crew to begin cutting up the huge timbered frame into boiler-sized chunks of wood. For the next two years, the Barbey boilers generated steam made possible by Henry Barbey's imagination and ingenuity.

The interior of the Barbey Packing Co. salmon cannery at Flavel
(Photo courtesy Columbia River Maritime Museum)

As an afterthought, he had the plant engineer salvage all the ironwork left after the timbers had burned, and this was sold for junk later, netting Barbey more than he had paid for the wooden hulk.

When the 1919 salmon fishing season opened, the Barbey Packing Co. of Flavel was ready, and canning operations began as soon as the first shipment of freshly-caught salmon arrived at the Terminal dock. That year, the salmon fishing season ended on August 24. It had been a good one for most of the salmon packers who collectively put up a total of 506,000 cases. The packers had paid eleven cents a pound and had sold the pack at a wholesale price of $13 a case. Henry Barbey had put up the smallest pack on the lower Columbia River but it was a beginning. He had nowhere to go now but up.

The season's pack for the various salmon packing companies on both sides of the Columbia river are listed below:

Columbia River Packers Assn. — 120,000 cases
Union Fishermens Cooperative Packing Co. — 60,000 cases

Booth Fisheries — 28,000 cases
Altoona Packing Co. — 40,000 cases
Warren Packing Co. — 30,000 cases
Pillar Rock Packing Co. — 25,000
J.G. Megler & Sons — 30,000 cases
Tallant-Grant Packing Co. — 45,000 cases
Sanborn-Cutting Packing Co. — 35,000 cases
McGowan & Sons — 35,000 cases
Chinook Packing Co. — 40,000 cases
Barbey Packing Co. — 10,000 cases

The new cannery at Flavel was a success from the beginning although Henry Barbey had to face difficulties like every other businessman, but he had a problem which most of the others did not have. He was very young to be the head of a large salmon packing company and was aware of it himself. In an attempt to look older than he really was, he began to wear a derby hat, thinking that the dapper topper gave him a more mature look. Early employees recall Henry Barbey driving up to the Flavel cannery in his Stutz Bearcat and wearing that famous derby, looking for all the world like a movie star arriving at the studio for a day of shooting.

It was at about this time that he began calling the men "boys" and the women "girls", not because he looked down on them but because he was simply unable to remember most individual names. Henry Barbey was a pleasant, courteous man and was invariably polite to everyone but his intense ability to concentrate on problems facing him made him appear distant and formal on most occasions.

One employee remembered an occasion when Henry Barbey was watching the unloading of a scow full of salmon from one of the seining grounds. The salmon was dumped loosely into the scow at the seining grounds to haul it to the cannery dock. The men at the cannery would have to get down into that cold slimy mass of fish and, using a fish pew, a stick about the size of a broom handle with a sharp steel pick on the end, would pitch the individual salmon from the scow into a dump box which was hoisted onto the dock where they were placed into salmon carts and taken either into the cold rooms or into the cannery for immediate butchering and canning.

All of the men pewing the salmon had been taught to stick the fish in the head instead of the belly because if stuck in the belly the fish would bleed internally and spoil the flesh. On this occasion, Henry Barbey was watching an inexperienced worker, obviously in his sixties, pitch the salmon. After seeing him make several sloppy stabs with the fish pew, Barbey could contain himself no longer. "You there, boy," he shouted. "Stick those fish in the head, not in the belly." The older man looked up and saw the dapper young man in a derby hat staring angrily down at him from the dock above. He was about to put Barbey in his place when one of the other workers quickly warned him that it had been the big boss talking. The older worker went back to his task with a red face but now watching where he pewed the salmon.

In addition to his own problems of supply, production and sales, Henry Barbey, as the owner of the cannery, had to face and solve many other problems which constantly came up during the production season. Many of these seemed trivial at the time and yet taken together, they created a constant challenge to him to keep his employees happy and production high and constant.

One such problem came up which seemed to be a minor matter at the time and yet was of enough importance and significance to be remembered by Mrs. Christine Hendrickson Loback after almost sixty years.

"It was a good place to work," she said, "but back in those days we had no union and we had to speak up whenever something was done that we didn't like."

"In the cannery at that time there was a big clock on the wall right over the retorts and the girls on the salmon line used this clock to tell them the correct time. There were no regular 15-minute rest breaks then and the girls used to go to the restroom all at about the same time each morning and afternoon. It was soon noticed that the line seemed to stop production at about the same time each day so the big clock was removed and a wooden clock put up in its place. The hands on this clock showed only the time when the fish cooking in the retorts should be taken out and could not be used for the actual telling of time."

"This action did not set at all well with the girls who felt that their rights had been trampled on. At lunch that day, they all met out on the lawn in front of the Flavel Hotel to eat and to discuss the problem. Most of them were highly indignant at having their clock removed and refused to go back to work when the whistle blew signalling the end of the lunch hour."

It wasn't long before Henry Barbey was notified that the salmon girls were not at their stations so he came hurrying out to see what the problem was. "What's the matter with you girls," he said. "Why aren't you working on the salmon line this afternoon?"

Mrs. Loback laughed as she remembered what happened then. One of the girls whose name was Ina had a very squeaky voice and she got up and said, "We're not going to go to work because we are human beings and we want real clocks, not wooden ones. Real clocks!"

"That's right," the others said indignantly. "We're humans and we demand real clocks on the wall."

"Real clocks!" Ina squeaked again.

Henry Barbey laughed. He knew about the wooden clocks but had not realized that anyone would object to them. He went into the cannery and ordered the wooden clocks taken down and a real wall clock installed in their place over the retorts. Then he returned to the group of ladies lolling on the lawn. "All right, girls," he said, "you have your real clock to look at. Can we all get back to work now?"

Getting and keeping good help was a constant problem at Flavel. It was a small town and there were not too many young women available for work so Henry Barbey had to go to Astoria and find additional help there. One of the women he found there and persuaded to come and work for him at his Flavel cannery was a young girl named Christine Hendrickson.

"I was working for Arthur Anderson at the time," she said, "and Henry Barbey stopped me one day and asked me if I would come over to Flavel and work for him. I had been working for Arthur Anderson since 1915 but he paid piece work wages and Barbey said he would pay hourly wages so I decided to leave the Anderson cannery and work for Barbey."

When asked how much she received doing piece work, Christine, now Mrs. Loback, replied that Arthur Anderson paid $1.25 cents for labeling one thousand half pound cans, and $1.35 for labeling a thousand one pound cans. All labeling at that time was done by hand instead of by machine as was done later. "Sometimes we worked for a dollar a day or even less," she said, "so Mr. Barbey's offer sounded good to me."

When the unions came into the canneries, piece work wages were abolished and other benefits put in including regular morning and afternoon coffee breaks. Uniforms were also provided free for all employees. Before this, each person had to provide his or her own uniform including rubber boots when needed.

Christine Hendrickson was willing to go to work for Barbey but she still faced the problem of traveling to and from the cannery each day to her home in Astoria. In those early days, roads in Clatsop county were few and were for the most part very poor. From Astoria, one had to drive around Smith Point, cross Youngs Bay on the old wooden bridge and then drive along the dikes to Miles Crossing. From there, the road led to the Lewis and Clark River, across the tide lands, now a part of the airport, and then to Warrenton and Flavel. It was a long, hard trip but it was the only way to get from Astoria to Flavel.

"I had an old car then — Hupmobile — and Mr. Barbey said he would give me a dollar a day for each girl I could bring with me over to Flavel to work. We got six girls together and we all left Astoria each morning about seven and got back home again twelve hours later."

The following year, there were more girls wanting to work for Barbey and Christine's car was too small to carry so many girls so Henry Barbey hired Jake Bosshart, a Warrenton woodyard owner, to take his wood truck over to Astoria each morning to pick the girls up. Each evening, he would haul them back to Astoria again, all riding in the back of the open wood truck.

"We would all meet in one place each morning in Astoria," Christine said, "and Jake would pick us up there. It was an old truck with wooden sides and one of those hand cranks for dumping the wood out so it was not too comfortable but as long as the weather was good, it wasn't a bad way to travel."

Mrs. Christine Hendrickson Loback, who is ninety now and lives in a comfortable apartment at the Clatsop Care Center, chuckles as she recalls those early days. "I was only about twenty-three years old at that time. I left Norway in 1906 and had been working in canneries since 1915 so I was used to it. I was only fifteen when I started so I had to get a permit from the state to work. I liked Henry Barbey and stayed there for several years. I can remember he and Mrs. Barbey would bring the baby down to the plant sometimes to watch us work." The "baby" was Graham Barbey, the Barbey's only child, who must have been about a year old at the time.

"I never saw the baby but I did see Mrs. Barbey a time or two", Alfred Johnson said. Mr. Johnson is eighty-one years old now and lives in Naselle, Washington, but when he was a boy, he worked for the Barbey Packing Co. at Flavel. "The Barbeys lived in the Flavel Hotel at that time and she came over to the cannery occasionally."

He chuckled as he recalled how he got a job with Henry Barbey. "I was living at Hammond in 1920 and I had heard that there were jobs to be had at Barbeys so I walked over there to see if I could get on. I was only thirteen at the time but tall for my age and I thought I could fool him into thinking that I was about sixteen. The first couple of times I went in, Henry Barbey wouldn't hire me because he thought I was too young."

"I was determined to get a job there so I kept going over to the Barbey plant. I had to walk about four miles along the railroad track each way but I was young then and didn't think anything about it. Well, about the fourth time I went in, Mr. Barbey looked at me and said, 'Now, Alfred, how old are you really?' "

"I tried to look very sincere as I lied, 'Sixteen, Mr. Barbey, I'm really sixteen.' "

"I don't think he really believed me but this time he grinned and said, 'Okay, Alfred, you can start to work here if you really want to that much.' "

"I really enjoyed the summer I worked for him," Alfred Johnson said. "I did a little of everything a kid could do. I would put the cans in the rack before they went into the retort and then when they came out again — they were hot — but after they cooled I would put them into cases — 48 in each, and then piled them up for a truck to pick up later."

"I did quite a bit of cleaning up. I used a broom and swept all of the dirt and debris down through the cracks in the floor into the river below. I would pick up things and toss them overboard too. In those days, everything we didn't want went into the river but it never seemed to get to shore. I guess the suckers, carp, and the seagulls got it all."

"I liked Mr. Barbey very much. He was a tall, well-built man, as I remember, with a pleasant personality. He was always fair in dealing with the people around him. Every day, he would make his rounds and take the time to talk to the workers."

"He brought the checks around himself and gave them to the workers because he liked them and that was one way of seeing and talking with them. I think I made about two bits an hour so that check could not have been too big but when you are only thirteen, it is pretty exciting to get a paycheck from the big boss."

"I liked working there," Alfred Johnson said. "There was always something to see or do. I can remember all of those Austrian purse seiners coming in and lining up at the dock while they delivered those huge loads of salmon."

"At lunchtime, we all went out on the dock to eat. As I recall, that summer of 1920 was a hot one and it was nice out there. I would have a fishing line and after I ate my lunch, I would fish off the dock. I would always catch a few suckers or tom cod but I wouldn't keep them. I just enjoyed catching them."

"You know," Alfred Johnson said as he looked back over sixty-eight years, "I worked at the Pillsbury mill at the Port of Astoria years later and Henry Barbey had his cannery right across the street, but I never did go over and see him. I wanted to remind him of how he had hired a thirteen year old kid to work for him back in 1920. I wish now that I had."

It is significant to observe that much of Henry Barbey's success was due to his ability to get along with his employees. Most of them have remarked that working at the Barbey canneries was a pleasure. He was one of the first salmon cannery owners to pay his employees by the hour instead of by their individual production, and always insisted on providing comfortable facilities for the worker's comfort and well-being. He moved easily through the cannery during working hour, rarely criticizing but always observing, although in an unobtrusive manner. If the employees had a complaint, they went to him rather than to a hierarchy of bosses.

Occasionally, a former employee has remarked, "I left Barbeys once and went to another cannery to work but I didn't like it as well so I went back to Barbey. He always treated us well."

It is easy to see why Henry Barbey made such a success with his cannery at Flavel and later at Astoria. He was a good boss.

Chapter 6

THE FIGHT TO SAVE THE PURSE SEINERS

Henry Barbey was satisfied with his first year's operation but there were still problems facing him which would have to be solved if he was to stay in business as an independent salmon packer. First and foremost was the need to establish a permanent and dependable source of enough fresh salmon to keep his new cannery operating. To do this, he had to depend to a greater extent on the independent fisherman than did the larger packing companies. For the most part, they had large groups of gillnetters bringing in salmon to their docks because they had earlier contracted to deliver salmon there in return for loans for nets, boats, and winter living expenses.

Henry Barbey had no gillnetters under contract. He owned no gillnet boats and made no advances to gillnetters as did many of the other canners. His method was to pay cash to whoever would sell him fish. Since the contracted gillnetters could not ethically do this, he had to buy almost all of his salmon from purse seiners, trap fishermen, and from trollers. Of course, there were always gillnetters who needed cash and would sell off part of their night's catch before going in to the docks of the Astoria packers with what they would claim was their full catch for that night. Many gillnetters felt that they were independent once they had paid off their indebtedness to the cannery which backed them, and then were free to sell to the highest bidder the rest of the season.

There is no doubt that the actions of the independent fish buyers hurt those salmon packers such as the CRPA which financed their gillnetters with loans made before the season even started. They depended upon these gillnetters to deliver their catches intact to the CRPA receiving scows or to the main cannery, and any salmon sold off the top to independent fish buyers cut into their total volume.

Fred Barker, manager of CRPA, was constantly frustrated by the inroads made by Barbey and others into his total salmon deliveries and complained often in letters to his brother W.H. Barker of the British Columbia Salmon & Fishing Co. about this problem.

"In our own case, we will have to adopt some different measures, as I am satisfied our fishermen will not deliver us their fish unless we come up nearer the price of the cash buyers. There is no money in doing this, but at the same time we cannot afford to be idle. What I am getting at is this, that it would be a very hard matter for us to go on a cash basis, as our men depend on us to keep them going during the winter months, and furnish them supplies. We have so many stations where these men live, and this all counts for something."

"We are up against a mean class of competition, especially around Ellsworth and St. Helens. The Barbey Fish Co. is paying fourteen cents straight and Joe Burke is doing the same thing. Klevenhusen is paying, we understand, as high as fifteen cents for what few fish he is getting. Our price to the fishermen, as you know, was twelve cents."

"The Barbey Fish Co., even now, is paying fourteen cents per pound, around Puget Island. When it is considered that his buyer's commission and freight to his cannery at Flavel will make his price sixteen cents, I cannot figure how he will come out even."

It is rather amusing to see how Fred Barker's opinion of Henry Barbey and his fish buying tactics changed through the years. In the beginning, during those first years when Barbey operated out of Portland and was not important on the local fishing scene, Barker tended to downgrade his activities to his fish buyers and associates.

In 1916, C.C. Ruckles of the Doty Fish Co. of Kalama, an associate of CRPA, wrote Barker about the local fishing scene. "I told our buyers to tell the men that we would allow them ten cents from the opening of the season, the same as the other packers did. I did not like to do this, but it was either do that or lose practically all our men. They say that Barbey is paying eleven cents. I do not know anything about it, it is only hearsay."

In reply, Barker said, "I put the matter squarely to Mrs. Megler that as far as Barbey was concerned we paid no attention to him, and that her actions, if she was standing in with Braim was a different matter entirely."

There were some things CRPA could do to keep their contracted gillnetters in line and the company did not hesitate using any leverage they could put on the fishermen to keep them from selling any salmon at all to Barbey and to others buying from gillnetters. Fred Barker wrote to the manager of the Altoona station concerning one of these fishermen.

"Regarding George E., some of his people bailed him out, and while his niece was in the office, she inadvertently let fall the remark that he intended to operate the other boat and deliver the fish to Mrs. Henry, fish buyer for Barbey. Please see that this is not done, otherwise we will take away our friend's gear entirely, and he will not be able to operate or fish for anyone."

The introduction of the salmon purse seiners on the Columbia River suddenly created a new source of fresh salmon for the packers and fish buyers on the lower river. Few of the purse seiners were affiliated with any established salmon packer and were free to sell their catch to the highest bidder. The independent fish buyer with his supply of ready cash was able to go directly to the boats and buy their catch each day. He was in a good position to get most of the purse seiners' fish. For the first time, the independent packers and buyers had access to all the fish they wanted and were able to compete on a better basis with the established old-line packers. It was probably for this reason that the big packing firms fought so hard against the purse seiners and were instrumental in drawing up legislative bills which ultimately drove the purse seiners from the fishing scenes on the Columbia River.

The Barbey Packing Co. dock at Flavel with the purse seining boats unloading. About 1920.

Purse seines had been used on Puget Sound for many years but did not appear on the Columbia River until 1905 when an Ilwaco fisherman adapted his boat to use a purse seine. It was highly successful and his example was soon followed by others.

Fishermen from Puget Sound soon heard about the success of the Columbia River purse seiners and began to come south to use their equipment to fish for the Chinook salmon in competition with the river gillnetters. Most of these men were of Austrian descent and at the time of World War I feelings against these fishermen ran high since most Americans at that time were in sympathy with the Allied forces fighting in Europe. Because Austria was an ally of the Germans, it was automatically an enemy of the Allies. Perhaps some of the local fishermen who seized upon this patriotic device as a means for getting rid of the Puget Sound purse seiner had selfish motives for doing so.

The fact was that the purse seiners were just too successful. They fished the same waters as the gillnetters did, but individually took a much larger share of the available salmon than the gillnetter.

Purse seiners unloading at Flavel.

The reaction of the gillnetters and the Astoria packers was swift. In 1917, a bill was enacted which prohibited the use of purse seines within the three mile limits at the mouth of the Columbia River. There was, however, no penalty attached to the bill and it did not eliminate the purse seiners to any degree. In 1919, another bill was drawn up by the Oregon legislature attaching penalties to the former bill and this second bill effectively eliminated the purse seiner from the Columbia River.

A hearing on the proposed purse seining bill was scheduled to be held in Salem on February 6, 1919 and many Astorians planned to attend. Astoria, at that time was probably the second largest city in Oregon and its citizens were able to put considerable pressure on pending legislation because of the long-time wealth and power of the Astoria and Lower Columbia fishing and packing industry.

On this particular issue, however, Astorians were divided into two camps. On one side were the gillnetters and their supporting packing companies while on the other stood most of the independent packers and the purse seiners. The two opposing sides were not equal, however, because most of the purse seiners were from Washington and had no base of local support while their backers, the independent salmon packers, were generally small companies without the wealth and resources of the giants of the industry.

To make the battle more lopsided, almost all of the upstream salmon packers from Astoria to The Dalles had come out against the purse seiners. A far-sighted few could see in this battle to eliminate one form of salmon fishing, future problems facing other methods of fishing such as fishwheels and seining grounds. If the purse seiners could be taken out of the fishing competition on the Columbia River, why couldn't the seining grounds and the fishwheels face the same fate in the future?

Henry Barbey, only thirty-five years old but already regard-ed as a "comer" by many segments of the salmon industry up and down the river, was one of those Astorians who attended the hearing. His Barbey Packing Co. of Flavel was only a year old in 1919 but he had been a prominent member of the buying and packing fraternity since 1912 and his business acumen was well known in both camps. This was the first time, however, that he had actually attended an official hearing on any pending salmon fishing legislation so he was regarded by many of the more mature packers and fishermen as an unknown quantity. He traveled to Salem in February 1919 to present his arguments against the pending controversial legislation and turned what had been planned as a peaceful hearing before the committee on fisheries into a violent confrontation between himself and Albin Norblad, senator from Clatsop County, and future governor of Oregon.

When his turn came to testify against the proposed legislation, Henry Barbey stood up and took his place before the assembled committeemen. They saw a mild-looking man of medium height, already greying at the temples, and dressed immaculately in a tailor-made suit. He was not impressive in physical appearance and yet his controlled manner and quiet well-modulated voice caught the instant attention of the committeemen.

They expected to hear a balanced, calm appraisal of the possible situation which could develop if the purse seiner legislation passed the Oregon legislature but instead they were startled to hear Barbey open an attack which exceeded anything expected from such a mild appearing man. The words caught their immediate attention and left them breathless.

"This bill was introduced in the interests of a so-called gillnetters' union at the mouth of the Columbia River and for a certain bunch of packers on the Columbia River who want to see the purse seiners wiped out of business and the only available supply open for the independent packers done away with," Barbey said. He was referring, of course, to the gillnetters' union and to the salmon packers who had gillnetters under contract and who did not have to buy salmon from independent fishermen such as the purse seiners.

"The ways have been greased and well greased for its passage through this legislature," Barbey added. He waited, knowing that his words would provoke some kind of reaction from the assembled legislative members.

At this, Senator Norblad, chairman of the Joint Committee On Fisheries, jumped to his feet and shook his fist at Barbey. "Who got this greasing?" he shouted angrily. "What do you mean by coming before this committee with such insinuations? I want you to know that I drew this bill myself and that it was not done at the request of any union or of any packers either."

Henry Barbey stood his ground, unruffled. He turned to another member of the committee and said, "And as for you, Mr. Ballagh, if I was working for a fish company I surely wouldn't take a job on a fish committee." He was referring to the fact that Ballagh had a regular job with a salmon packer. As a matter of fact, E.I. Ballagh was in charge of the CRPA fish station at St. Helens and later became Master Fish Warden for the State of Oregon.

Representative E.I. Ballagh stood up and declared solemnly that he was working only for the State of Oregon at the present time and not for any salmon packer.

Barbey went on and charged that the bill penalizing purse seine fishing on the Columbia River had been framed in the interests of the Seuferts, the Sanborns, the McGowans, the Warrens, and other owners of Columbia River fish canning plants.

"The gillnetters want to hog it all," Barbey declared. "All available locations for other forms of fishing have already been gobbled up and the passage of this bill would deprive hundreds of fishermen of their only means of livelihood."

Senator Robert "Bert" Farrell representing Multnomah County, supported Barbey's contention regarding the selfish motives of the gillnetters and declared that the bill was unjust and unreasonable. "It is only a camouflage to put the purse seiner out of business," he declared, adding that such a step could only be the forerunner of the ultimate elimination of every type of fishing gear now used on the Columbia river.

Farrell, however, also had interests in the purse seiner controversy. In addition to being president of the Deep River Logging Co., he was also president of the Taylor Sand Fish Co., the Columbia Fish Co., and the Chinook Investment Co. He was, however, a very fair man and sympathized deeply with any fisherman out on the river battling the elements to make a living. He was also a far-seeing individual and could see a bleak future for the Columbia River packing industry if the various segments of the fishing industry began trying to eliminate each other in a vain attempt to get more than their fair share of the limited salmon resource.

"Why call it a camouflage?" Senator Norblad said. "There is no attempt to cover up the real motive back of this bill. I will frankly admit that the bill is designed to keep the purse seiners out of the Columbia river."

Senator Albin Walter Norblad had tied his future to the growth and power of Astoria since 1909 when he had arrived there with a young family and a law degree from the Chicago Law School. He had opened a law office in downtown Astoria, bought a house up on Grand Avenue, and had soon become an up and coming politician in the town. He had been named district attorney, circuit court judge, and was elected to the state legislature in 1918. He was to serve in the state senate until 1929 before becoming governor of Oregon in 1929 following the sudden death of Governor Patterson. He was not re-elected to the office.

During his years in Astoria, Norblad had thrown in his lot with the established salmon packers and had been vitally interested in legislation effecting the salmon industry. He had seen the growth of the purse seining fishing industry and could see that if allowed to grow, it would eventually hurt the gillnetters. There were thousands of gillnet fishermen in Clatsop county and very few purse seiners so it was natural enough that a rising politician would throw in his lot with the larger group. Norblad was an honest man but certainly biased in favor of the gillnetters. He was also the attorney for the Union Fishermen's Packing Co.

Peter Grant of the Tallant-Grant Packing Co. of Astoria told of his objection to the proposed penalties to the purse seiners, saying that the law as it now stood imposed a physical impossibility upon the purse seiners and that is why it was unjust legislation.

Other fishermen attending the hearing added their objections. One stated that as high as $14,000 had been invested by one fisherman in equipment for purse seining and that the enforcement of the law as proposed would practically wipe him out of business.

It was a hopeless fight and Henry Barbey knew it. By 1922, the legislatures of both Oregon and Washington enacted laws to exclude purse seines from the Columbia River. One of the main sources of salmon for the Barbey Packing Co. had thus been eliminated.

There is no doubt that the purse seining bills were originated and backed by CRPA and other large packing concerns. Fred Barker said in a letter, "The purse seine case was decided in our favor about two o'clock the same day the case was heard, the 25th."

In another letter, he said, "So far, we have been able to keep the purse seiners from fishing. Four of them were arrested by the Washington deputy aboard the Oregon patrol boat. They were put under $500 bonds, and their trial was to have come off last night."

Even after Oregon outlawed the purse seiners, the CRPA kept up the pressure to eliminate them from Washington waters as well. In another letter, Fred Barker said:

"Sept. 29th and 30th, I went over to Seattle, together with Henry McGowan and Al Gile of the Chinook Packing Co., Senator Sinclair of Pacific county, and our own man Hawkins from Ilwaco. We had an interview with the Washington Board of Fisheries, to the end of trying to get them to pass an order to conform with Oregon prohibiting purse seining in what they call the Willapa Harbor district. This is immediately opposite Seaview or North Beach right where the purse seiners operate. It is claimed they do not do any fishing in the waters controlled by the State of Oregon, that is fishing outside the Columbia River, although they do fish outside the North Jetty, but this is in the State of Washington."

Henry Barbey was not about to go out of business just because one group of his suppliers was being eliminated. In April, 1919, the *Pacific Fisherman* reported that the Barbey Fish Co. was putting in improvements for the convenience of fishermen at various points, and would have a large scow at the jetty sands ready to buy salmon for cash at highest prices. During that second year, the Barbey Packing Co. of Flavel put up 22,950 cases of salmon in the spring pack.

The Barbey Packing Co. of Flavel, even with the elimination of the purse seiners, was on its way.

Chapter 7

SAND ISLAND

Sand Island! Even today when that sandy bit of land in the middle of the Columbia River is useless to all concerned and is little more than a small piece of sandy, grassy land protruding above 200 square miles of muddy river water. The mere mention of the name can still create fierce arguments as to its legal ownership.

The State of Oregon has taken the federal government to court in a fight over who owns or controls the island. The State of Washington has tried to take it from the State of Oregon. The Indians have consistently maintained that they rather than the white men have the right to fish the island. The gillnetters have tried to force the seining ground operators off. The salmon canners have fought each other for years over the right to use it as a base for their fishing operations, and finally, the Columbia River has nibbled away at it for years, taking a bit here and there, and at times depositing more land than it takes. It is a wonder there is anything left at all of Sand Island.

Today, Sand Island is a grassy, deserted spot of land situated just south of the Washington shoreline almost within the confines of Bakers Bay. It is legally owned by the State of Oregon but is physically within the State of Washington. In any case, it is virtually useless for all practical purposes.

In the beginning, Sand Island was a part of the State of Oregon and the Oregon Territory. At the time the boundaries of the new State of Oregon were drawn in 1859, Sand Island lay nestled close against the north edge of the state. The main channel of the Columbia River ran north of the island.

This was the situation during the early Civil War days when the commandant of Vancouver barracks near Portland

Aerial photo of the mouth of the Columbia river taken in 1929 by Brubaker Aerial Surveys of Portland. At lower left is Clatsop Spit with the south jetty cutting through it. Cape Disappointment is top center with the north jetty leading out from it, fringed with surf. Sand Island is just to the right of Cape Disappointment with Peacock Spit just to the left of it. (Photo courtesy Columbia River Maritime Museum)

designated the island as a strategic point for military fortifications for guarding the entrance to the Columbia River. He requested President Lincoln to withdraw the island from entry by homesteaders so that it could be saved for military purposes. Lincoln consulted his advisors and found that the island belonged to Oregon and could not be withdrawn.

Undaunted, the commandant petitioned Governor Gibbs of Oregon to cede the island to the federal government. Gibbs requested the state legislature to do so and, in deference to the governor, the legislature did just that. With the gift, however, they put in a clause which said that the island was to be used for military purposes only. The federal government took control of the island but the Civil War came to an end and just about everyone concerned forgot about the island.

At one time, a man named Johnson decided to homestead the island and was about to file the papers when the commander of Fort Columbia on the north side of the Columbia River notified him that his gunnery crews used the island as a target and that if Johnson attempted to build a cabin on the island, he would be blown to kingdom come. Johnson decided to homestead in a quieter location and that was the end of that.

During all of these years, Sand Island was on the move. The powerful currents of the Columbia River had for many centuries kept the island tight against the shoreline of Oregon, but when the jetties were built at the mouth of the river, the currents changed and suddenly began running south of the island, cutting away at the south side and adding to the north side. Gradually, the island moved northward toward the State of Washington, and by the turn of the century was close to the Washington shore.

For many years, no one cared who owned the island or where it was. As long as most of the salmon were caught by gillnetters, the island was of no importance. Once the idea of catching salmon by the use of seines caught on, Sand Island suddenly became important. Most of the seining grounds were under water at high tide, but parts of Sand Island were always out of the water and it was located immediately adjacent to the main current of the Columbia River where the bulk of the salmon run passed. Suddenly, Sand Island became the most valuable fishing ground in the Pacific Northwest.

Now everyone wanted Sand Island. Someone in the War Department, realizing the value of the island, conceived the idea of leasing the fishing rights on the island to the highest bidder. A yearly bid was scheduled and fishing rights were given to whoever bid the highest amount for those rights. Money began pouring into the US treasury for these rights, much to the delight of the United States War Department.

Oregon looked on with dismay. Why should all of that money go to the Federal Government when the State of Oregon could use it for better purposes? State officials looked into the Sand Island leases, noted the clause which stated that the Federal Government could only use the island for military purposes and sued to regain the island. They claimed

Seining at Sand Island.

logically enough that seining ground leases were not primarily for military purposes. This argument dragged on through various courts for many years.

The State of Washington eyed the revenue from the seining ground leases too and decided that it wanted them. The state sued for possession of the island, claiming that it now belonged in Washington since it was situated less than a mile from the north shore. To prove this claim, a number of Washington residents waded over to it one day without getting wet above the knees. In 1908 the boundary was definitely fixed by the courts as running north of the island, thus putting Washington out of the running for the seining ground revenue. This decision stated that the north channel of the Columbia River ran north of Sand Island, disregarding the fact that a rowboat could not navigate that channel at low tide.

Eventually, the courts held that Oregon owned Sand Island and that the Federal Government had no right to lease the seining rights on the island. By this time, seining on the river had been outlawed and once again Sand Island was useless for all productive purposes.

In 1919, at the time Henry Barbey first set up the Barbey Packing Co. at Flavel, Sand Island was one of the most important fishing grounds on the Columbia River. For many years, the larger packing firms had bid on the five seining sites on the island for relatively small amounts of money. They dominated the industry and were used to having their own way.

In 1915, for example, the Columbia River Packers Assn. bid on three of the five seining sites of Sand Island. Amounts bid were $589 for Site No. 1, $7,898 for Site No. 2 and $2987 for Site No. 3. W.E. Tallant bid in on Site No. 4 for $1750, while George Davis of Chinook bid $605 for Site No. 5. Each of these bids was for one year's use of the site. The successful bidders had the right to use the sites for five years, renewing the lease at the amount bid each year. Every five years, the government asked for new bids on the five sites and at these times, others could submit a bid to use one or more of the Sand Island sites for salmon seining purposes.

With the elimination of the purse seiners, Henry Barbey had to find a new source of salmon. Most of the seining grounds were owned by individuals or by packing companies, but the Sand Island seining sites would be up for bids in 1925 and then would be tied up once more for another five years. If he could get one or more of those sites, the Barbey Packing Co. would have a good supply of fresh salmon each year until 1930.

Henry Barbey had already leased other seining grounds on the river. He had the lease on Welch's Sands and had a crew each year working it under Brick Miller, seining-grounds foreman, but the salmon he got from there was not enough to keep his packing company going. He had even tried earlier to set up his own seining ground at the mouth of the Skipanon river near Warrenton, Oregon, using Chesley Smith as his seine foreman, but he soon found out that there was such a dropoff there, the seine could not drag the bottom and the salmon escaped under the net so he was forced to give up that idea.

He had already submitted a successful bid for Site No. 3 on Sand Island in 1922 against CRPA and had won the site with a bid of $6,789. His crews had fished that single site of 3500 feet of beach on the south side of Sand Island successfully for three years, but Barbey realized that a truly successful seining operation on the island required a larger area for operational purposes. Even so, the salmon his crews brought in from Site No. 3 helped keep the Barbey Packing Co. operating during the early part of the 1920s.

It should be noted here that each of the five seining sites on Sand Island was approximately 3500 feet long, running from west to east. Site No. 1, adjoining the dry part of the island, was at the western end and Site No. 5 lay on the eastern tip. Sites No. 2, 3 and 4 lay between these two. All faced to the south where one of the main channels of the Columbia River was located, and all seining was done along this stretch of beach.

Henry Barbey was a gambler but one who looked carefully at all aspects of the gamble before he made a move. He had studied the history of the Sand Island bids and knew who would be in the bidding and the approximate figure each could be expected to submit as a bid.

A new element had entered the fight for Sand Island in the form of a newly-formed seining ground on Peacock Spit. For many years, the Spit had been simply a rock formation at the mouth of the Columbia River but after the north and south jetties were built, sand began building up around Peacock Spit and it soon became possible to use drag seines on the new sands.

In 1923, Bankers Discount Corp., which was owned by the former Tallant-Grant Packing Co., applied to the War Department for the privilege of seining on Peacock Spit but were turned down on the grounds that a new seining grounds at that location would interfere with Sand Island operations. They also said that the run of salmon did not warrant leasing of further seining privileges.

This decision did not stop McGowan & Sons, a Washington salmon packing firm, which obtained a seining license from the State of Washington during the following year and started seining operations there in July. The post commander of Ft. Stevens, who assumed jurisdiction over the new sands,

Seining at Sand Island.

ordered McGowan off his military reservation but McGowan came back with the argument that he was fishing with Indians who had a prior right to fish there.

Somewhat dryly, Fred Barker of CRPA said later, "The facts are that this Indian crew was fishing for McGowan on shares, presumably 50/50, and they have fished for McGowan in the past, McGowan bringing down this same crew from an up-river ground that we formerly owned near Rooster Rock, where fishing has not been profitable."

At this time, CRPA was assuming that it would get the leases on the Sand Island seining sites as they had in the past. In a letter dated July 19, 1924, to A.B. Hammond, the major stockholder of CRPA, Barker said, "We, together with others, have fished on Sand Island beach for the past number of years, and we will bid on these sites next year in order to get our supply of fish. Should McGowan, through any means, be able to fish on Peacock Spit, it would break up the schools of salmon and would make seining operations on Sand Island beach less valuable. Would it be possible for you to lay these matters before Major General Morton, of the Presidio, San

Francisco, to the end that fishing not be allowed on Peacock Spit?"

At the time he wrote this letter, Barker didn't dream that CRPA would ever lose its leases on the Sand Island seining grounds but he had reckoned without the redoubtable Henry Barbey.

It was time for his grand move. On February 23, 1925, Henry Barbey turned in bids on each of the five seining sites on Sand Island. His bid was a surprise to everyone and when the amounts of the bids were announced, the surprise turned to consternation. He had outbid all competitors on each of four sites and had tied for the fifth, and, since he had won four out of five sites competitively, he had the primary advantage and was awarded the fifth one as well, even if his bid had only tied the competitors.

The bids were as follows:

Site 1 — Barbey Packing Co., $7,790; CRPA and Sanborn-Cutting Co. (a joint bid) $7,575; Alex Miller, $50.

Site 2 — Barbey Packing Co., $22,690; CRPA and Sanborn-Cutting, $18,575; Alex Miller, $1,900.

Site 3 — Barbey Packing Co., $11,250; CRPA and Sanborn-Cutting, $9,575; Alex Miller, $700.

Site 4 — Barbey Packing Co., $3,500; CRPA and Sanborn-Cutting, $3,500; Alex Miller, $600.

Site 5 — Barbey Packing Co., $500; Alex Miller, $80.

The prices bid on that day were the highest ever paid for the Sand Island seining rights. Henry Barbey had put up almost a quarter of a million dollars for the right to use the five sites on Sand Island for the next five years. It was a grand gamble.

Now, Sand Island was all his. By outbidding the other firms, Henry Barbey had won the right to control for five years the most valuable seining ground on the Columbia River. Given the proper fishing conditions, the returns from those grounds could be large and if so would ensure the continued operation of the Barbey Packing Co. of Flavel.

One can only imagine the consternation in the higher echelon offices of CRPA and the other packing giants caused by the news of Henry Barbey's successful bid. The upstart independent salmon packer who only six years before in 1919 had managed to pack only 10,000 cases of salmon compared with CRPA's pack of 160,000 cases, had actually outbid them and was now in a position to control and harvest the best salmon seining ground in the world. It was suddenly apparent that Henry Barbey of the Barbey Packing Co. was a man to watch if they wished to continue their tight control of the salmon packing business on the Columbia River.

Fred Barker of CRPA, in an obvious attempt to minimize the loss, wrote to W.H. Barker about Barbey's success in the leasing of Sand Island. "I do not know if it has come to your attention or not, but Barbey has leased all five sites on Sand Island for a period of five years. They will cost him approximately $48,000 a year. The highest I ever paid for sites one, two and three was $14,000, and for the past three years we only had one ground and caught 700 tons in three years, and our rental for each year was $6680. One of the grounds, No. 1, has washed away entirely. This is the one we had last year, and No. 5 is of very little use, so it practically only gives him three grounds. The best ground, No. 2, looks as though it is going the way of No. 1. This is immediately abreast of the *Great Republic* wreck. The *Republic* is now in very deep water, and the seining nets never reach it, showing how the island has receded."

Barker added at the end of his letter: "Barbey has also leased Chris Schmidt's cold storage plant, so he is spreading out a good deal, and taking more chances."

Suddenly forgetting about their protest to A.B. Hammond about McGowan using Peacock Spit for seining on the grounds that it would hurt seining operations on Sand Island, officials at CRPA took another look at the Spit and decided that perhaps it should be seined — but by CRPA and not by McGowan.

The Bakers Bay Fish Co., a small Washington fish company controlled by CRPA, obtained a lease from the State of Washington for the Peacock Spit seining ground and then promptly sold the lease to CRPA in an apparent bookkeeping transaction. All lease costs and operating charge were to come out of the sales value of fish caught on the grounds.

Looking ahead five years, CRPA, then under the new management of W.L. Thompson, who was tired of watching Barbey reap the immense salmon harvest of the island, went in with Henry Barbey and submitted joint bids for the Sand Island seining sites in 1930. The giant and the upstart had apparently reached an agreement as equals. It must have been a satisfying occasion for Henry Barbey.

He had reasons for going in with CRPA on Sand Island in 1930. For one thing, under the new agreement, CRPA would get half the catch on Sand Island but the Barbey Packing Co. got half the catch from Peacock Spit so Barbey came out about even on the deal.

Barbey was willing to dicker with Thompson in 1930 simply because Sand Island was not as good a seining ground then as it had been in 1925 because of a singularly odd circumstance. In 500 B.C., the Greek philosopher Heraclitus said that you cannot swim in the same river twice, and today that could be changed to mean that you cannot fish in the same river twice either because the Columbia River changes constantly. The currents, tides, winds, and floods were constantly changing the river and consequently the channels and the sands. Each tide and each day the sands would change a bit and from season to season, they could change a great deal so each year was different. A seiner never knew what condition his sands would be in at any time.

Even so, seiners can usually rely on their sands remaining in a condition where they can be fished, regardless of changes. An event, however, occurred at Sand Island unexpectedly which changed its character forever. After it happened, the Sand Island seining grounds were never the same again.

In 1928, an American schooner *North Bend* was inbound from Australia when her captain attempted to cross the Columbia River bar without a pilot and the ship stranded herself on Clatsop Spit on the Oregon side of the river. Salvage attempts were made to free her but nothing worked so she was abandoned and left to the elements.

For a year, the *North Bend* lay on the sands, exposed to wind and sea, but suddenly she freed herself and spent some time moving about near the mouth of the river before moving over to Sand Island where she was beached once more and again was abandoned, but the *North Bend* was not dead yet. Pushed by the winter winds and currents, she began to move across Sand Island, cutting a channel as she moved. Eventually, she reached Bakers Bay where she refloated herself, thirteen months after she first was stranded on the Spit. The resurrected *North Bend* was then purchased and converted into a barge and was used for many years in that form.

This exploit of the *North Bend* was so extraordinary that it was featured in Robert Ripley's "Believe it or Not" column which was very popular in those days.

It was bad news for Sand Island and for Barbey, however. By cutting a channel through Sand Island, the North Bend changed the character of the island and virtually destroyed a good portion of the seining grounds there, so that by 1930, they were not as valuable as they had been five years before.

Back in 1925, however, Henry Barbey had stuck his neck out. He had the seining sites, but, as the *Astorian Budget* commented at the time, "There are circumstances which are ungovernable and which make bidding upon the fishing rights on the island a hazardous gamble."

The newspaper was referring to such factors as the weather, floods, strikes, the price of fish, future legislation, and other problems which continued to plague the fishing industry.

Henry Barbey had thrown his hat across the river with a vengeance. He had gambled his entire future on Sand Island and would have to "go across the river to get his hat" or go down to defeat. Henry Barbey, however, was not a man to go down without a fight. He intended to get that hat!

Chapter 8

NEW FIELDS TO CONQUER

Is there such a thing as being too successful too soon? Henry Barbey was probably wondering this after returning from his annual vacation in California, ready to face the 1925 salmon packing season. 1924 had been a good year for him but it had also brought a new set of problems which had to be faced and soon.

When he had leased the Hill Terminals at Flavel in 1919 for use as a salmon cannery, the facility had been perfectly adequate for his needs at that time. Then, the Barbey Packing Company had depended for the most part upon salmon purchased from the purse seiners and from his buying stations at Ilwaco, Hammond, and Chinook. From past experience, he had been able to calculate almost exactly how much salmon he would be able to buy and had set up his cannery to operate at that production level.

By the spring of 1925, however, everything had changed. The purse seiners were gone now and that source of freshly-caught salmon had disappeared forever. He still maintained his buying stations but that source alone could not supply his needs and was too uncertain at any given time. To get salmon there, he had to pay a higher price to gillnetters than their home plant was paying, and he had to convince the trap fishermen of Chinook, Washington that they should sell to him and not to other independent buyers.

By obtaining the seining leases on Sand Island, Henry Barbey had eliminated for at least five years his reliance on these uncertain sources of salmon. He now had the best seining grounds in the world and given five average years of seining he knew that the Barbey Packing Company would be able to put up a much larger pack then ever before. This was the new problem. How could he put up a large pack using the Flavel facilities when they were designed for a much smaller operation?

There were three possible answers. First, he could simply pack as many cases as his present cannery could produce and then close up for the rest of the year. That possibility, he dismissed instantly. In bidding for the Sand Island leases, he had guaranteed a rental which over a period of five years would total more than a quarter of a million dollars. If he limited his pack, he would not be able to make the yearly payments and would lose the leases.

A second possibility was to modernize the Flavel plant and make it more productive so that the total catch from Sand Island could be packed. The lease on the Hill Terminals, however, included a clause giving the S.P. & S. the right to terminate the lease on six months' notice. If that happened for some reason, he would have to pack up the cannery and move it to another location, possibly right in the middle of the canning season. This option was unacceptable to Henry Barbey.

No, the only possible alternative was to build or acquire new packing facilities elsewhere. He knew that he did not have time enough before the salmon fishing season began to build a new cannery but he could possibly get another place to handle part of the catch.

Immediately after winning the Sand Island seining ground leases, he had contacted Fred Barker at CRPA on March 19, 1925, asking him if CRPA would provide ice for his newly-expanded operation. "Each trip you deliver us ice," he said, "we will take from 10 to 20 tons, so that you would not have to bother with frequent deliveries. We understand that this ice comes in 300 pounds cakes and is to be delivered to our dock at Flavel at $5.00 per ton delivered."

Swallowing his pride and wanting to salvage something from the loss of Sand Island, Barker agreed to furnish ice to the Barbey Packing Co. "You need to have no fears of not being able to get ice from us during August and September, or at any other time. We will deliver from ten to twenty tons each trip, so you will not be bothered with frequent trips."

Barker, however, did turn Barbey down on another request he made which may have helped mollify his sense of frustration at losing Sand Island. Henry Barbey, on March 19, 1925, the same day he asked for ice, also requested something else from CRPA.

"You have five new Sand Island seines completely hung and these seines were hung for Site #2. By lengthening these seines, we can use them on #4. I would pay you the market price of these seines plus a small allowance for the labor of hanging them."

Barker replied: "We have a deal on for the use of these nets, and should we sell them now, we would have to order new nets ourselves. But thank you for your offer."

It is obvious that Fred Barker's deal which was on for the use of the Site #2 seines was to be on the new seining sands on Peacock Spit, which CRPA through its subsidiary the Bakers Bay Fish Co. had recently leased.

At least, Henry Barbey did get his ice from CRPA which was something. Ice, in the salmon packing industry is an absolute necessity. Fish delivered at the cannery must be iced immediately to retain its freshness. Many times when deliveries came in so fast that the butchering and canning crews were unable to handle it all, the excess salmon would be iced down and kept fresh until the crews could get to them. His Flavel operation simply was not adequate for producing this quantity of ice, once the Sand Island catch began to come in to the cannery docks.

The Barbey Packing Company canned salmon but it also processed mild cure salmon, and froze a part of the catch. If the mild cure and the quick freeze portion of the processing operation could be done elsewhere, the Flavel cannery could probably handle the canning of salmon caught at Sand Island. It would be tight but some of the pressure would be off, at least for 1925 and 1926.

When Henry Barbey made up his mind to do something, he moved rapidly. In April of 1925, the *Astorian Budget* announced that the Barbey Packing Co. had leased the cold storage plant of S. Schmidt and Company in Astoria. Even though it was unhandy to have the two packing facilities as far apart as they were, the added space of the S. Schmidt building gave him the flexibility he needed to handle the huge catch of the Sand Island seining grounds.

Barbey moved the frozen fish operation and the mild cure to the Astoria plant and used the space gained at Flavel to put in new machinery and storage. Additional men were hired for both plants and a new delivery schedule was set up so that salmon from Sand Island could be sent either to the Flavel cannery or to the S. Schmidt plant at Astoria on the *Mayday,* his new cannery tender, or by his other receiving scows.

The new system worked very well for the 1926 salmon season. Henry Barbey packed more than 50,000 cases of salmon which that year was second only in volume to CRPA's pack of 80,000 cases. In addition to the canned salmon, Barbey had also put up 400 tierces of mild cure salmon and 200 tons of frozen fish. The many other salmon canneries along the lower Columbia river had been hurt that year by a gillnetters' strike which had lasted twelve days and consequently had cut the total catch for the season. This loss had been disastrous for the salmon canneries which depended upon the contract gillnetters to supply them with salmon to can. The strike actually helped Barbey because the Sand Island seining grounds were kept open during those twelve days and caught many of the salmon which might otherwise have ended up in a gillnet.

To demonstrate the sheer volume of salmon needed for processing a profitable pack for the year, it should be pointed out that 32.5 tons of raw salmon were needed to pack each 1,000 cases of canned salmon which meant that Barbey had to have more than 16,250 tons of salmon for his 50,000 case pack in 1926 or 3.25 million pounds of raw salmon. If each salmon averaged 40 pounds, this meant that his seining ground crew had to catch 812,500 salmon for the pack.

That was just for the canned salmon. In addition, Barbey put up 200 tons of frozen fish and 400 mild cure tierces which substantially increased his needs.

A tierce is a barrel which contains more than 300 pounds of processed mild cured salmon. To mild cure a salmon, the

The Barbey Packing Co. fish receiving station at Rainier. In the
background is the Longview bridge.

Chinese crew picked out the big prime salmon with no gaff
marks on them. The heads were cut off and the fish cleaned
but the tails were left on the carcass. Each salmon was
then cut in half lengthwise and the backbone removed.
These pieces of raw salmon were packed carefully into the
tierces in layers until the barrel was full. A combination of

water and salt was then poured over the salmon and the filled tierces were put aside for a month after which the brine was poured off and a new mixture of brine added. This process was repeated three times and then the final brine was left in and the barrels sealed. The mild cure process was over and the filled tierces were ready to be shipped to Copenhagen for the European market. This processed salmon was a very desirable commodity in Europe and commanded a high price there. It was a profitable sideline for the Barbey Packing Co. even if it involved a time-consuming process.

The following year Henry Barbey expanded his operations again but this time up the river and out of the Lower Columbia area. In April of 1927, the *Morning Astorian* announced that the Barbey Packing Co. had purchased the Allen & Hendrickson plants and interests at Rainier, Oregon, a small town about fifty miles east of Astoria.

The Allen & Hendrickson plant had been operating for twelve years at Rainier, packing salmon as well as fruits and vegetables. It was located on the waterfront at Rainier and had a dock with deep water for bigger boats, an ideal setup for use with Barbey's *Mayday*, now captained by W.C. Lester with Ralph Edwards as engineer. These two with Henry Barbey went to Portland just after the Rainier cannery was purchased, and bought a new gasoline launch for use at the two canneries.

In 1931, the Rainier site was the scene of one of the few disasters Henry Barbey suffered. In September of that year, the *Mayday*, now captained by Ralph Edwards, was struck by the bow of the steamship *Florence Luckenbach* while the cannery tender was enroute from Rainier to Astoria in a dense fog with a large load of salmon. The steamship was traveling downriver at a good speed, powered by her engines and also by the current. She struck the *Mayday*, rolled her over, and put a large hole in her bow. Capt. Edwards and one crewman, Robert Sigurdson of Astoria, managed to save themselves by clinging to the wreckage, but a second crewman, Victor Teir, a teenager from Rainier, was drowned.

The Barbey Packing Co. cannery tender Mayday *prior to her rebuilding after the collision with the Luckenback ship at Rainier. (Photo courtesy of the Columbia River Maritime Museum)*

Bob Sigurdson later told his brother Clarence what had happened. "It hit the *Mayday* like this — plopped her upside down and the keel of the *Luckenbach* dragged the keel of the *Mayday* and she kept on going over and back up again and she floated. She dumped 25 tons of fish in the river and that's the reason she got hit. They stacked so much fish up on the deck that it was hard to see out of the pilot house window. When we left Rainier we saw the *Luckenbach* up the river coming down but we figured — we misjudged the timing — we figured we would be across the river before the *Luckenbach* reached that point."

"But one of the bad things was that the *Luckenbach* did go past the channel and was over on the Washington side when she hit the *Mayday* which was already past the main channel."

Clarence Sigurdson continued the story. "Bob said he was

the last one to get out of that pilot house and he was scrambling around and finally he got out but before he got to the surface of the river he had taken in some water. It happened that when he got to the top of the water, there was a fish box there and he got his arm over it and held on. There were fish all around and then the *Luckenbach* stopped and sent a lifeboat back."

"Everyone was looking for the kid. Bob said that he would dive down after he got his breath and would feel all over and he thought he had him but it was a salmon. The water was full of salmon. He would let go the salmon and go down again but they never did find the kid until the next day."

Ralph Edwards, the captain, thought the boat was right side up and went out the pilot window but when he reached up to give himself a shove, he realized that he was shoving himself further down. He grabbed the whistle and gave it such a hard yank — it was an air whistle — he broke it off. There was 175 pounds of air in the tank and the released air shot Edwards to the top like a bullet."

By a strange coincidence, Bob Sigurdson's sister Anna had taken a bus from her home at Seattle and was traveling to Warrenton to see her family. The bus was just crossing the river at about that time and when they got to the bus station at Rainier, Anna heard that the *Mayday* had been the boat struck and that somebody was missing. Knowing that her brother was the engineer on the *Mayday,* Anna left the bus and stayed over in Rainier. Much to her relief, she found out that her brother had been saved and was there to welcome him the next day.

Tier's death cast a pall over the Barbey operation. He was only eighteen and had just started working for Barbey on that day. He had chosen to take the job of assisting with delivering the 25 tons of salmon aboard the *Mayday* to the Barbey Astoria plant rather than attend a dance in Rainier the same night because he felt that he needed the money.

The *Mayday,* although badly damaged, did not sink and was towed to a Rainier drydock by the towboat *Nadine* of Longview. While there, the *Mayday* was almost completely rebuilt and never looked the same as she did before the tragic collision with the *Florence Luckenbach.*

The Allen & Hendrickson company began business in Rainier in 1917, starting small and canning only salmon, employing only twelve to fifteen people. In 1918 they began packing the evergreen blackberry, later adding fruits and vegetables. The cannery took up the canning of beans in 1922, the first year's pack amounting to only 500 cases, while in 1926 the pack reached an impressive 60,000 cases. A total of more than 500 workers were on the payroll of the company.

The new plant added to Barbey's capacity for canning and gave him a few other advantages as well. For one thing, he bought the labels formerly used by Allen & Hendrickson and used these, not only for the vegetables and fruits, but for his salmon as well. "Pride of Oregon" had been used on some of the finer grades of string beans so it was also used to create a new brand for a better grade of canned salmon.

It may be noted here that labels are a valuable commodity to any packer. A great deal of thought goes into finding new names for canned products and subsequently designing a label which will reflect that product favorably.

There are two types of labels: packers and buyers. When one is starting out, it is less expensive for a packer to sell to a buyer under the buyer's label in which case the cost of advertising is up to the buyer. It is expensive to advertise and takes many years to develop your own or what is called a packer's label, as the cost of advertising and promotion is up to the packer.

Henry Barbey started out by selling most of his canned salmon pack to New York buyers such as Seaman Brothers, Francis H. Leggett, Krasne Brothers, and the other large wholesale grocers who had developed their own labels.

Later, he developed his own labels. He used Barbey Supreme Brand on his Fancy Chinook Salmon, Mayday brand on his Choice Chinook Salmon, Columbia Kist Brand on his standard Chinook Salmon, and Springtime Brand on his Fancy Shad Roe and Kippered Sturgeon.

Although he sold part of his pack under his own brands, Henry Barbey sold a major portion of his yearly pack through the years under buyers' labels. Some of these were S & W, S.S. Pierce, 1st National Stores, Beacon Importing, Kroger,

Merchants Importing Colonial Stores, Star Markets, Ralph's Markets, and Safeway Stores.

One Seattle canned salmon broker developed a label in the New York market over a period of fifty years which was called Red Breast Salmon. This was Fred Gosse and he used this label mainly on ocean caught coho salmon which were medium red in color and sold at a popular price in the New York market. When Fred Gosse decided to retire, the Barbey Packing Corporation purchased this label from the F.A. Gosse Co. This was a major sales assist to Barbey as the Red Breast Coho label was a major label in the New York market at that time.

The author, who was an employee of the Barbey Packing Co. during summer vacations while attending the University of Oregon, remembers working on a labeling crew. The Chinese crew did the hand labeling of oval cans, and the round cans were labeled by a crew running a labeling machine.

Each lot of salmon was given a code on the lid of the cans so the contents would be known by the company. It would tell the date, contents, and grade of salmon in each can.

The buyers liked to see the letter "A" on the cans — they thought that that meant "good". The packers always put A's or B's on the cans and never X's or Z's because if they used these letters, the buyers would think it was poor-quality salmon.

It was interesting to the author to find that portions of the same lot of salmon might be sold to three different buyers so that different grocery stores could have the same code lot of salmon under different labels. In other words, if S & W and S.S. Pierce, both top quality buyers, bought parts of the same lot of spring Columbia River Chinook salmon from Barbey Packing Co., a housewife could possibly find in her local gourmet grocery store that both a can of S & W Columbia River Fancy Chinook Salmon and a can of S.S. Pierce Red Label Columbia River Fancy Chinook Salmon had the same code on the top of the can.

The brand name "Mayday" was chosen because the finest quality of salmon on the Columbia River was caught during the month of May. Henry Barbey called his number one grade Barbey Supreme and his number two grade or "Choice" as it was called in the industry, "Mayday".

He also named his biggest cannery tender (pickup boat) the *Mayday*. During World War II, the word "Mayday" was used as a distress call so after that the boat *Mayday* could not have a ship to shore radio and use the name "Mayday".

The new Allen & Hendrickson plant had been packing more than 40,000 cases of string beans in addition to their other packs. This string bean was a new variety which had been developed by Oregon State College and was an innovation because it had no strings. It was called the Refugee Stringless Bean. It also grew well in the Rainier-Claskanie area and was the one packed under the "Pride of Oregon" label.

Acquiring the Rainier facility brought Henry Barbey into a new field far from the salmon he knew so well, but he inherited the manager of the plant, A.E. Allen, who had been in charge of the plant from its inception and who continued in the capacity of manager of the Rainier operation. The company, under his direction, purchased the seed and contracted with farmers in that area to grow and deliver the string beans to the cannery. The beans were delivered to the cannery by truck, and were dumped into large metal vats that had thousands of small holes or mesh. These vats rotated and the beans were washed and the ends would fall through the mesh and be cut off. They were then graded as to size and quality, put into cans and cooked in a retort. After cooling, they were labeled, boxed and shipped to such wholesale grocers as Mason, Ehrman & Co., Wadhams, General Grocery, and others for distribution.

Barbey's new Rainier cannery also packed jams and jellies made from local berries when they were in season although Henry Barbey decided to send the strawberries down to Astoria rather than can them at Rainier as had been formerly done. He ran these through his quick freeze in barrels and shipped them out for the hotel, restaurant, and soda fountain trade.

Looking ahead many years, Oregon State College developed a new variety of string bean called Blue Lake string bean which proved to be superior to the Refugee Stringless bean canned by Barbey at Rainier. Unfortunately, this new variety grew better around Salem where it wasn't as damp as it is in the Rainier area so Barbey stopped canning string beans and used the cannery as a fish receiving station only. Eventually, the Allen & Hendrickson canning plant was abandoned and Henry Barbey donated both the buildings and the waterfront property to the city of Rainier for one dollar. It was a valuable piece of property measuring two city blocks facing the river and fronting on the downtown district of Rainier and the donation was welcomed by the citizens of Rainier.

In spite of the new problems of running the unfamiliar Allen & Hendrickson cannery at Rainier, Henry Barbey managed to put up a 55,000 case pack of salmon at Flavel, surpassing his 1926 pack by 5,000 cases. He also put up 200 mild cure tierces and a substantial frozen pack.

It had been a good year for Henry Barbey and the Barbey Packing Company.

Chapter 9

CRPA AND OTHER COMPETITORS

Through the years, there probably have been more than a hundred different canneries located on both sides of the Columbia River established for the express purpose of canning fresh salmon. Many of these have been small individual businesses while a few have been gigantic corporations, but they have all been set up for one purpose: to can the delicious Chinook salmon.

Each of these different canneries had to obtain enough raw salmon to warrant the expense of operating a cannery through the salmon fishing season. Each had to have a reliable labor pool available; each had to have a physical packing facility, and, of course, each of them had to be able to sell the finished product at a profitable price.

One of the giants of the salmon packing industry of the Lower Columbia area was the Union Fishermen's Co-operative Packing Company which was organized in 1896 by a group of gillnetters who were dissatisfied with the prevailing conditions in the industry at that time, and who realized that the only way they could change them was to set up and operate their own packing facility.

These gillnetters were looking for a fair return for the salmon they brought in and they were also trying to give the consumers the best salmon available under the name of the Royal Chinook salmon. They were tired of being at the mercy of the cannery owners and felt that if they had their own salmon packing cannery, they could bring some measure of control to the basic uncertainties of gillnetting on the Columbia River.

They had just come through what turned out to be a disastrous strike against fish prices gillnetters thought too low, and were ready to do anything possible to attain some kind of individual financial security on the river.

The first share of stock for the new packing company was sold to Thomas McFarland on October 14, 1896 for $100, and was signed by Charles Wilson, president, and Sofus Jensen, secretary, as officers for the new packing company. An issue of $30,000 of capital stock was issued.

Through the years, it has been said that the Union Fishermen's Co-Operative Packing Co. was set up primarily by Finnish fishermen but of the first ten shares sold, only half of them were sold to men with Finnish names. Many of the early subscribers were also Norwegians and Swedes so the new packing company was owned and operated by a number of different nationalities.

On January 16, 1897, work was started on the new cannery building on a site in Uniontown in the west section of Astoria. Uniontown, incidentally, is not named for the Union Fish cannery but rather is called that simply because the first residential district on that side of the Bond Street hill established in the 1880s was called the Union Addition, a name soon shortened to Uniontown.

A large packing plant measuring 50 by 200 feet was erected and adjoining boat moorages and net racks were built by the stockholders themselves. On April 11th of that year, 191 sailing gillnet boats brought their salmon to the new facility for the first time.

The preparing and canning of the salmon was done mostly by a Chinese crew, hired through the contracting system then in effect at most of the Astoria canneries. It was hand work for the most part but the new co-op put up a sizeable pack that first year, enough to ensure the continued operation of the Union Fish cannery, as it was called.

During its second year of operations, Union Fish established the two labels which became famous through the years as a leading brand of canned salmon. "Gillnetters Best" and "Cooperators Best" began to appear on cans of salmon being shipped to all parts of the country.

Through the years, Union Fish extended its operations, building receiving stations, warehouses, bunkhouses, cold

Tourists admire the big salmon in Barbey fish boxes on the packing company dock.

storage facilities, and by increasing the size of its original building. Eventually, it became one of the largest salmon packing operations in Astoria.

Even though the co-operative began to add to its pack by buying salmon from trollers and from trap men, it never used the seining grounds as a major source of fresh salmon, depending almost entirely on its gillnetting stockholders to bring in enough fresh salmon to keep the cannery operating.

Union Fish, as it was usually called in Astoria, had an unusual problem because it was owned by the cannery workers and the men who fished for the cannery. Each one of them more or less considered the cannery and everything in it as their personal property. After all, they said, "We own it, don't we?"

People who worked for the Union Fish and were not stockholders said they often resented the constant pressure from fellow workers who were stockholders to work harder and keep longer hours. "Everyone was a boss," they said.

Pilferage was a problem at Union Fish as it was at most of the local canneries. A can of salmon and later albacore tuna was a small item which would fit easily into a purse or coat pocket. If 200 workers each carried home a can a day, that cannery had automatically lost many cases of canned salmon and consequently a considerable amount of money.

Henry Barbey followed an iron-clad rule regarding taking any fish, canned or fresh, from the cannery. Jim Ferguson, a former employee and manager, tells about it: "The thing about Henry was that he had some good rules. One of them was, never take any fish for yourself without paying for it. Even when he took a case of salmon home, he always charged himself. When his son Graham took a case home, he always paid for it. Even when he took a case of tuna to his mother, he charged his mother for the fish."

"Henry's reasoning was to never take samples without paying, because if your employees see you take the sample, they'll do the same. When you are dealing with high priced things such as salmon, tuna, or kippered sturgeon, a can is worth a lot of money."

This policy must have cost Henry Barbey a considerable sum of money during the years he operated his canneries because he was known by all of his relatives and friends as a generous man and very few of them ever visited the Barbey Packing Co. without leaving with a gift case of fish, courtesy of Henry Barbey.

"Henry Barbey was always careful about his money and was always getting the last nickel out of a piece of equipment." Jim Ferguson said. "When I was working on a truck or something, he would come out and say, 'Well, Jim, it has worked for 40 years. I don't know why it can't work for another forty.' "

"When we were replacing planks in the dock, he would come over and say, 'Well, Jim, do you think you can turn this one over and use the other side?' "

"That was a big factor in his success. He watched his pennies and the dollars took care of themselves. I admired this in him."

The giant of the salmon packing industry was the Columbia River Packers Assn., commonly known as CRPA. It was formed in 1899 when seven of the major salmon packing companies of the Lower Columbia region joined forces in a new corporation, consolidating ten different canneries. Such early packers as Samuel Elmore, J.O. Hanthorne, B.A. Seaborg, J.W. Cook, George H. George, William H. Barker, and M.J. Kinney joined the new packing company and elected William Barker general manager. The plan developed was to use only three of the canneries thus eliminating duplication of many of the cannery functions. Sam Elmore, a former mayor of Astoria, was a vice-president but served as manager until his death in 1910 at which time George H. George took over. He died in 1913 and was replaced by Fred Barker.

One of the major stockholders of the CRPA was A.B. Hammond, railroad man and lumberman, and founder of the town of Hammond. The widow of Sam Elmore also owned a large percentage of stock in the company. These two rarely participated in making decisions about the cannery although Hammond's expertise in the field of banking and finance was used for the advancement of the huge packing company.

In October of 1924, it was announced that William L. Thompson and W.A. Tyler had purchased the stock interests of A.B. Hammond and of the Elmore estate thus making them the majority stockholders in the corporation. The deal, which involved nearly two million dollars, also took in the stock of William Barker.

W.A. Tyler was the president of the Astoria National Bank while William L. Thompson was the vice-president of the First National Bank of Portland. The following day at a stockholders meeting, William L. Thompson was elected president of the corporation. A new era had come to the Columbia River Packers Association.

Included in the physical assets of CRPA at that time were the big packing plant at Astoria as well as a cold storage and refrigeration plant. There were other canneries at Ellsworth and Eagle Cliff, Washington, canneries at Nushagak and Chignik, Alaska, two ships Tonawanda and Chillicothe besides many small boats, eighteen receiving stations, and a large number of trap sites, seining grounds, and fishing rights along the Columbia River. The labels including the famous Bumble Bee brand were listed in the sale as one of the primary assets, as indeed they were.

Thompson was a tough operator and soon was known in Astoria as a man who knew what he wanted and would get it if he could. He made many enemies in the area and in the industry but he was able to keep the company afloat during difficult financial times. He was the head of the largest salmon canning company on the Columbia River and did his best to run all of his competitors out of business.

It was not long before he was nicknamed "Tule" Thompson by almost everyone on the Astoria waterfront although no one ever dared call him that to his face. A tule, for the uninitiated, is the local name given to one of the old hook-jawed salmon that live in the deep holes in the Columbia River. They are usually big, heavy fish, slow-moving and yet very powerful. W.L. Thompson once suggested to his fishermen that the fall-caught Chinooks be graded and paid for according to quality — so much for the brights and less for the pale or tule grade. This suggestion earned him the nickname "Tule" Thompson.

One of Thompson's main targets when he first came to town was Henry Barbey. Thompson took over CRPA in October of 1924 and less than six months later, he had to face the fact that Henry Barbey, one of the smallest of the independent packers, had actually come in and outbid the mighty CRPA in the fight for the Sand Island seining ground leases. Barbey had taken over one of the best fishing grounds on the Columbia River and would have fishing rights there for five years — a seining site which CRPA had held for many years before Barbey had shown up on the river. One can imagine Thompson's wrath over this sudden turn of events.

And yet, Henry Barbey's bold move was the kind of audacious maneuver that Thompson admired. Riches and prestige are for those who have the ability and boldness to go out and get them and he admired any man able to do that.

Strangely enough, W.L. Thompson and Henry Barbey became good friends in a very short time. They were almost complete opposites. Barbey was quiet and unassuming while Thompson was noisy and blustering, but they enjoyed each other's company and soon were playing golf together, and on weekends the two families would get together for a game of bridge.

The Barbey home at Gearhart, Oregon in 1932.

It was a strange relationship, however. Graham Barbey said that he could recall W.L. Thompson suing Barbey and Henry Barbey suing Thompson all week long but on the weekends, the Thompsons would be houseguests of the Barbeys at their Gearhart home and they would all have the best of times. Thompson's wife Alletta and Ethel Barbey were good friends and frequently traveled together hunting antiques.

Certainly, the two men discussed business along with pleasure and, even though they were competitors, did manage to compromise and cooperate when there was a necessity to do so. Obviously, in the matter of the Sand Island seining ground leases in 1929, the two men did agree to cooperate rather than fight.

Luckily, Henry Barbey had a placid disposition and plenty of patience or he could not have gotten along with the flamboyant and tough-talking Thompson for one minute. Thompson's manner of speaking to subordinates and employees was hard to take and for a competitor to have to listen to this type of thing was almost impossible. Henry Barbey, however, got along fine with Thompson, even at the worst of times.

Graham Barbey relates an account of one of Thompson's meetings he attended which illustrates Thompson's almost brutal attitude towards others. The salmon packers of Astoria and the Lower Columbia area met frequently to discuss industry problems, and one of these meetings was held in Thompson's office at the CRPA. Present were John McGowan and his uncle, H.S. McGowan, one of the owners of McGowan & Sons of Ilwaco, Lawrence Rogers of Point Adams Packing Co., Arthur Anderson, head of Columbia River Salmon Co. and Graham Barbey, representing his father for the Barbey Packing Co.

Also present were Thompson's son Edward Thompson, Tom Sandoz, vice-president in charge of sales at CRPA, and Jim Cellars who had been hired away from the *Astorian Budget* by Thompson to handle labor negotiations for the packers. During the discussion, there was a disagreement about who was at fault for some of the problems of the industry. Thompson was angry about the problem of fresh fish buyers getting some of CRPA's share of the catch. He turned to Graham and asked him how come the Barbey Packing Co. was buying fish that belonged to CRPA.

"As a young and inexperienced college boy," Graham said later, "I was not used to being jumped on, especially by a man who was frequently a guest in my father's house so I told him to ask my father."

Thompson snorted derisively and said, "Why ask him? He's a goddamn liar anyway."

At this, both Jim Cellars and Thompson's son tried to stop him from going on but Thompson turned on them furiously and told his son to shut up or he would be fired, and told Cellars the same would go for him. He added to poor Cellars bewilderment by asking where he would be if Thompson had not hired him from his $1.50 an hour job at the *Astorian Budget*. Then Tom Sandoz tried to get in a word but was also told to shut up. At that, the meeting broke up in total discord and Graham Barbey returned to his father's office to relate what had happened. To his surprise, Henry Barbey chuckled and told him not to let old Thompson bulldoze him. "He'll calm down", he said. He was familiar with W.L. Thompson's tantrums and never allowed himself to get upset by them.

The following weekend, the Barbey's had as their houseguests at Gearhart William L. Thompson and his wife Alletta. They were all playing bridge and having the nicest time as if the meeting had never taken place when Graham Barbey arrived with a college friend, John Latourette Jr.

"John was a bit of a joker", Graham said, "and he told Thompson that he owned one share of CRPA stock and was wondering when he would receive a dividend on his investment."

Thompson stared at young Latourette for a moment and then reached into his pocket and pulled out a fifty cent piece which he tossed to the surprised youth. "Go away, boy. You bother me," he growled in his best W.C. Fields imitation.

According to Graham, W.L. Thompson often tried to get Henry Barbey's goat by offering Graham jobs at CRPA for more money than he claimed Henry paid Graham. "Come to work for me, kid," he would growl, "and I'll pay you what you are worth."

Physically, Henry Barbey and W.L. Thompson were almost completely different. Thompson was not too well as he was greatly overweight, looking as Graham Barbey said later, "somewhat like Winston Churchill." He ate too much, drank heavily, and smoked expensive cigars. Barbey, on the other hand, was trim, well-dressed and neat, ate sparingly, and did not smoke. Nevertheless, the two men did hit it off and remained friends and competitors for many years.

It is interesting to realize that three of the men at that memorable meeting in Thompson's office later became presidents of CRPA: Edward Thompson, Tom Sandoz and John McGowan.

Despite the above, W.L. Thompson was a smart business-man who took over the CRPA when it was in serious financial trouble. He carried it through the depression years, during which time, he was the largest employer on the Lower Columbia River, according to Graham Barbey.

In 1930, another canning competitor entered the field when New England Fish Co. purchased the Pillar Rock cannery, buying at the same time three fish receiving stations, and three seining grounds at Taylor Sands, Columbia Sands and

Farrell Sands. The sale also included three fish traps and a large block of stock in the Miller Sands seining grounds. It was obvious that from that time on, New England Fish Co. or NEFCO as it was commonly called, would be a force in fishing on the Lower Columbia River. Eventually, they had a cannery at Astoria and their operations there soon became an integral part of cannery row on the west side of Astoria.

In 1920, Point Adams Packing Co. was founded by C.L. Rogers, Ed Beard, Dick Fulton and Grover Utzinger. Pt. Adams had its headquarters at Hammond. Incidentally, there had previously been another Point Adams Packing Co. which eventually became a part of CRPA.

Arthur Anderson was another local independent salmon packer who operated the Columbia River Salmon Co., often confused with CRPA. Generally, Astorians simply referred to the independent cannery at the foot of Fourth street as Anderson's cannery. Anderson operated his cannery for many years but kept out of the public limelight and consequently was not as well known as some of the other cannery operators. Over-expansion for the albacore tuna eventually caused his operation's demise, which was then taken over by John Tenneson, a Seattle man with two salmon canneries in Alaska.

It would be impossible to give a full listing of all the salmon canneries that ever operated on either shore of the Columbia river. They were organized, sold, merged, and closed during the years from the 1880s to the present time with few of them leaving any kind of a lasting mark on the history of the salmon industry.

All of them are gone now and will never come back again. The buildings have been burned or torn down and the owners and operators are dead or have gone into other fields of endeavor. There is little left now of these great canneries which were an important economic factor in the Lower Columbia area.

Chapter 10

SEINING ON SAND ISLAND

In April 1925, Henry Barbey and his new Sand Island seining ground foreman Chesley Smith went out to the island to look it over and make plans for the coming fishing season. By getting the five year lease on this seining ground, Henry Barbey had taken over one of the finest fishing grounds in the world but he had pledged a quarter of a million dollars in lease money and knew that the next five years would either make or break him.

His first move had been to hire Chesley Smith to run the seining grounds for him. He knew that the 45-year-old foreman was the best on the river and that was what he wanted — the best. Out there on Sand Island, Barbey would not be able to personally supervise the fishing operation so he knew that he had to have a man he could depend on. Chesley Smith was that man.

Chesley David Smith was born in San Francisco in 1880 and came to Astoria with his mother in 1895 after his father had died. He went to work on a seining ground when he was fourteen as a general helper. He worked hard and learned all aspects of seining-ground work until he got his first job as a foreman on Kaboth Sands in 1903, working for the Tallant-Grant Packing Co. During the next few years, he was foreman at Meehan Sands, Tongue Point Sands, Welch Sands, and Miller Sands. Earlier, Barbey had hired him for a short time when he had attempted to seine the Skipanon River, an enterprise that had failed because of the rocky bottom and steep sides of that river. Sand Island, however, was different and it is easy to see why Henry Barbey chose Chesley Smith for his foreman in 1925 to run his new seining ground.

The two men tramped over the entire island, making notes of things to be done and of changes to be made. The seven mile long island was a desolate place at that time of the year. Most of it was just sand with half-buried driftwood logs dotting the landscape. The large end to the west had willow trees on it but to the east, it was all open dunes and wind-blown grass. It narrowed out to the east and it was along this stretch of the island that the channel was later cut through in 1928 which eventually destroyed the fishing grounds and rendered the island virtually useless.

In 1925, however, the island was in prime condition for seining but there was much to be done before the opening of the salmon season so Henry Barbey and Chesley Smith spent that day making plans for the coming season. There were men to be hired, and equipment and supplies to be purchased. There were buildings there already but many of them had to be repaired or even replaced, and new ones built.

Sand Island was a big operation. At one time, 160 men worked there with 66 horses, twelve seines, and many boats, cars and trucks although this number varied each season and even during the seasons. Housing and feeding this large number of men and animals proved to be a challenge to Barbey and Smith.

While most of the seining ground crew lived and ate on the island, those working the north end of the island were away from the others and lived and ate on a fish scow which was moored there across from Chinook, Washington. Here, board and room was furnished to ten Barbey workers who would take boats to the scow for the meals which were furnished by the cook Mrs. Frank Johnson and her helper Ida Lugnet. Lunches to go were provided by Mrs. Johnson who baked all of the bread used.

There were three camps on the island which were separated by about a mile of sand and shore but connected by a roadway which ran along the north shore. At the end of it was a dock where the cannery tenders such as the *Mayday* tied up to receive the daily loads of salmon. At the other end of this roadway were the bunkhouses, cookhouse, and other buildings.

Through the years, various salmon packing companies had held leases on the five seining sites on the island. At times, three different companies were operating on the island and each had to maintain its own buildings and other facilities. Many of these were temporary structures, designed to last for a year or so at the most but others were built for long-term use. If a packing company had used a seining ground for many years, it tended to constantly maintain and improve its own physical facilities. When Barbey won the lease on Sand Island, he found that he had inherited for a five year period, a variety of buildings and other structures already in place and, for the most part, useable. There were bunkhouses, barns, docks, cookhouses, net racks, and a kind of an office building already in place so he was able to move his crew and equipment to Sand Island with a minimum of expense.

Horses for pulling in the loaded seines were a basic necessity on all seining grounds. Boats were used to put the seines out and for bringing the salmon-filled seines in close to shore but teams of horses had to be used to bring the nets into shallow water and up to the beach. No salmon canner was willing to raise his own horses so a system of leasing the teams from individuals sprang up. There were a few of these on the Washington shore, including Allen Coulter, who provided teams of horses for many of the seining grounds including Welch's Sands, but one Oregon individual named Finley High successfully leased his horses to various seining grounds on the Columbia River for many years and was one of the primary sources of the horse teams used by Barbey.

Byron Fitzgerald, who now lives in Salem, Oregon, worked under Chesley Smith on Sand Island during those years. He said, "The horses we used were from Finley High and were good horses but we always had quite a time getting them broke to work in the water, but we found that the best way was to hook them to a log and make them sweat. In a week or so, they were broken."

At first, Finley High operated from the old Adair ranch near Warrenton. Vernon Hall, who now lives in Sweet Home, Oregon, worked for him during the early 1920s. In describing

One of the fish wagons at the Sand Island seining grounds. (Photo courtesy Byron Fitzgerald, Salem, Oregon.)

High's operation at that time, Mr. Hall said, "I drove teams for Finley High who rented the Dr. Owens Adair place, and shipped wild horses from Paisley, Oregon. We rough broke them for work on the various road jobs around Astoria. I received an extra 50 cents a day for driving his roughed horses until they were broken enough to be used on the seining grounds."

Apparently, Finley High moved his horse raising business eventually to Eastern Oregon. Riphath Christensen, who now lives on the Tucker Creek Road south of Astoria, told about his work with Finley High. "I worked for him when he had a ranch right out of Spray, Oregon, back in 1940. When we went there, we turned off at Arlington and went down through Condon and Fossil. That was a long old grind back in those

*The horse barn at the Sand Island
seining grounds. (Photo courtesy
Byron Fitzgerald, Salem, Oregon.)*

days. We left Portland about nine in the morning and got
into Spray about two in the morning. We had a little Chevrolet
truck and it pulled a semi which Finley was using to haul
the horses down to the river. He hauled eight to ten head
each trip. I think he got about $80 rent for a team for one
season. They were big boys — regular work horses."

"And it was that summer of 1940 that he lost two teams
out on the seining ground. We brought the pot of fish in
and there was a couple of big salmon that shot right out
there onto the sand, flopping their tails. It scared the team
and those horses took off then, got tangled up in the harness
and drowned. Finley High got paid for them later." Riphath
Christensen, looking back over the passing of almost fifty
years went on with his tale. "Now on Pillar Rock Sands, we
had a team run away. They were just coming down that

beach miles per hour so I says to a guy, 'You watch my team and I'll stop them.' Well, when they came by, I was going to grab that line but that horse saw my arm come out and she hit the other horse so hard they both rolled over." He chuckled. "One way or another, I stopped them anyway."

On Sand Island, there were barns for the horses but on many of the other seining grounds, there was just one big building perched up on pilings above the high tide mark and here the horse barn would be a part of the building so the horses and the men working the grounds more or less shared the same quarters.

Alfred Johnson, now retired at Naselle, Washington, said, "I didn't ever work for Barbey on his seining grounds but I did work for Kenneth Parker over on Phillips Sands which, I guess must have been a part of Van Dusen Sands. Anyway, at high tide it was all under water so everything had to be housed up on pilings. It was being leased by S. Schmidt at that time and they had a big building out there with a ramp leading up to it. The horses were kept in the first room which we had to go through to get to the rest of the building. Matter of fact, the eating area was right back of the horse barn but I can't remember any odor or any problem about that."

"Some of the men we had there were horse skinners from Eastern Oregon and they did most of the horse handling. They were a different type from the rest of us who were mostly college boys working through the summer but everyone seemed to get along real well. At least I cannot remember any fights."

Out on Sand Island, Chesley Smith and his wife Freda Jeldness Smith moved into a small house which had three rooms and an office. Usually, each seining ground had a small store which sold things such as candy, tobacco, gloves and waders, all items that the seiners needed during the season. Back in those days, each man had to furnish his own working clothes. During the day when Chesley was at work, Freda would tend the store.

In the early days, the men waded in the cold water in their regular clothing but eventually waders were invented and used from that time on. Waders are simply a waterproof

*Seining nets drying on Sand Island.
(Photo courtesy Byron Fitzgerald,
Salem, Oregon.)*

*Pulling in the seines at Sand Island. Chesley Smith was the seine
foreman here. (Photo courtesy Columbia River Maritime Museum)*

garment at that time made of canvas which covered the man's body from his feet to his chest. Later, the waders were made of rubber and were more efficient.

"We were forever patching those waders," Alfred Johnson said. "Almost every night, you would find a new hole in it somewhere — mostly where the legs rubbed together — and by the end of the day, you were about as wet as you would have been without them. They were expensive too. I think they cost about $25 which was four or five days pay so we tried to take good care of them but even so, at the end of the season we had to throw them away because there usually was very little left of them."

There was a large building on Sand Island called the clubhouse where the men ate. It was a long wooden building with an open-beamed ceiling. Inside, rows of tables ran the length of the room and were covered with oil cloth. All the food was served family-style by women waiters.

At Sand Island, the cook was Mae Woodfield, the widow of former seining boss Ernie Woodfield, who was assisted by two other women and a bull cook named Will Jones. Will helped with the heavy work, cut the meat, kept the fires up, and did the same jobs as the legendary bull cooks of the logging camps.

Every man who ever worked on a seining ground bragged about the food they were served. The men worked hard and ate heavily so the tables usually groaned under a big load of meat, potatoes, gravy, vegetables, and the inevitable pie. Calorie counting was not a part of seining ground life.

The seining ground tenders would usually bring a supply of fresh eggs, milk and vegetables each day but most of the supplies were landed at the beginning of the season and stored near the kitchen. Meat was kept in a cold room, cooled by big cakes of ice.

One of the problems facing the cooks was the constantly changing meal times. Each day, the tides were at different hours and, since the seining could only be done at the proper tide, each day the meal hours would change. On the days when the men began work at four or five in the morning, the cooks would have to have breakfast ready at three.

Complicating this was the fact that Chesley Smith was notorious for working his crew during the dark hours of morning and evening, and earned the nickname "Moonlight" Smith for this practice although none of the men ever dared call him that to his face.

Most of the men slept and lived in bunkhouses although a few of the boatmen such as Clarence Sigurdson slept on their boats rather than walk in each evening to the bunkhouse. The bunkhouses were simple wooden structures, sometimes two-storied, with rows of bunks down each side. Each man usually had a locker to keep his clothing and personal belongings in. Privies were generally outside but on the seining grounds which were under water at high tide, the privies were off the sleeping room and utilized the water below as a sewer.

As for baths, Alfred Johnson pretty well described the situation when he said, "I cannot remember any bathtubs or showers there. We got in on weekends and then most of the men would head for the Uniontown steam baths where they would get cleaned up. I suppose they did have baths for the women out there but I cannot remember anything for the men."

Fresh water was a problem on most of the seining grounds because there was no way to run a pipe out there nor any way to dig a well so all of the fresh water used had to be brought in or came from rain barrels placed around the buildings. Needless to say, there was no water to spare for unnecessary conveniences.

Many of the seining sites were a mile or more from the clubhouse so the men would often ride there on a sled pulled by the horse teams. On other smaller seining grounds, the men would simply perch on the team's doubletree and ride that way. Many of them went to the site on the boats used in seining. Walking in the heavy canvas or rubber waders was an unnecessary exertion and was avoided whenever possible.

Because there were five seining sites on Sand Island, Chesley Smith was not able to be at all of them at the same time so he had other foremen under him, each bossing different sites. Ernie Woodfield Jr., the son of the legendary Ernie

Sr., Brick Miller, and John Johnson were three he used on Sand Island. All of these men were experienced hands who could handle men and who were able to judge the tides, wind, currents, and other factors so as to take maximum advantage of each seine.

Chesley Smith handled one of the crews himself but often moved around the island, checking on the other sites. According to Riphath Christensen, Chesley used an old car — either a Model T or a Model A — to drive up and down the beach in. He had a piercing whistle which he made by putting two fingers in his mouth and blowing. It could be heard easily by anyone within a half a mile of Smith and was used by him frequently to call someone's attention to what was needed.

At the beginning of each fishing season, Henry Barbey was faced with the problem of finding a crew for his seining grounds. Chesley Smith remained on Sand Island for the full five years of the lease so Henry Barbey was always able to depend on him to run things, generally with the same under-foremen he had used in previous years although there was generally one or two vacancies in this category each year. Ernie Woodfield and Brick Miller both worked with Smith for those five years and then later, after Chesley had moved over to the Pillar Rock Sands in 1930, Woodfield took over as general foreman of Sand Island, working for both Barbey and for CRPA under their shared seining ground lease.

Many of the skilled people such as the cooks, engineer, and boatmen returned as did many of the previous year's workers but some of the college boys dropped out each year and these had to be replaced by others. There was always an inevitable turnover in other work categories so each year there were always some vacancies to be filled by new and inexperienced men. However, there were usually plenty of applicants for the seining ground jobs so Barbey always started each fishing season with a full crew.

Occasionally, there were more salmon caught than could be handled by the regular seining ground crew. In an interview which appeared in the *Daily Astorian* in 1974, George Kruckman, an early-day foreman on Desdemona Sands, told about a day when this happened during one of the years after 1930 when Barbey and CRPA were seining Sand Island together. Elements of the same story were remembered by other men who had been there on Sand Island on that day.

A solid wall of Chinook salmon entered the river that day and hit the seines on Sand Island. The crews there hauled the immense catches up on the beach and went back for more but it was soon obvious that there was more salmon there than could be handled so Ernie Woodfield, Barbey's Sand Island foreman at the time, put in an emergency call to Kruckman over on Desdemona Sands to bring his crew over to help. There were a hundred tons of salmon piled on the beach with more coming in and high tide was just hours away. The salmon would have to be moved off the beach before that happened or most of the catch would simply float away on the tide.

That day was an unforgettable one for the seining crews on the island. The fish started jumping and splashing even before the head buoy came ashore. One of the nets broke open and the men hurriedly laid another one around it to try and contain the mass of fish. Attracted by the huge run of salmon, a herd of sea lions had followed the big school in and had entered the seines with the salmon and were now busily charging back and forth inside the seine, biting the bellies out of as many salmon as they could seize. Rifles were hurriedly brought to the scene and the best markeman in the group began to pick off the sea lions before they could damage the seines.

As the loaded seines were dragged in, the salmon were simply stacked on the sand in high piles, waiting to be picked up by a crew with a horse-drawn wagon rolling along a plank road to the other side of the island where the dock was located. Ordinarily, the wagons could handle the seine catch but on this day, the fish were piling up faster than they could be moved.

"Every man on my island gave Woodfield's crew help," Kruckman said. "We worked until midnight moving fish. That was the biggest day's catch I ever saw on the islands." George Kruckman was interviewed when he was 82 years old and was at that time the oldest surviving seiner on the river.

The Barbey seining crew working at Welch's Sands off Astoria in 1937. Brick Miller was the seine foreman here.

Both crews worked tirelessly, loading barges and scows hurriedly sent over to the island from the two canneries. There was so much fish that fish boxes were piled around the edges of the scows and then the salmon were unceremoniously dumped in big piles inside of the ring of filled fish boxes. One of the scows was loaded so heavily that it partially sank but the crews managed to save most of the cargo of salmon.

The *Mayday*, Barbey's cannery tender, went back and forth between Sand Island and the cannery, hauling huge loads of salmon on its decks and towing the loaded scows behind. The *Toke Point*, another tender, was put into service as well and the two boats moved continuously back and forth across the river, trying to save as much of the catch as possible.

The salmon was delivered to both the Barbey and the CRPA canneries and were handled by extra crews called hurriedly to come to work as soon as the full scope of the huge catch became apparent. All of the gangs at both canneries worked around the clock for the next few days, trying to process the salmon before it could spoil.

In the folklore annals of the salmon fishing industry on the Columbia River, the day the "wall of salmon" hit the Sand Island seining ground stood out from all of the other days as one to remember by anyone who was there and saw that incredible catch. There had never been one like it before nor was there ever another like it again.

Henry Barbey seined on Sand Island for five years, from 1925 to 1930 at which time the government lease came up for renewal. By that time, the seining grounds there had been virtually ruined by changes in the island although some of the sites could still be fished. Barbey was able to look ahead at that time and realized that an individual bid on the Sand Island seining grounds could be risky so he hedged his bets and went in with CRPA on a dual bid for both Sand Island and Peacock Spit. In addition, Barbey leased the Pillar Rock seining grounds in 1930, thus providing his packing company with one more major source of salmon.

However, Henry Barbey's audacious bid in 1925 paid off for him and he was able to meet all lease payments each year and still make a very good profit from his Sand Island seining grounds as well as from his other fishing sources.

In 1926, the Barbey Packing Company put up 50,000 cases, 400 mild cure tierces, and 200 tons of frozen fish while in 1927, the pack was 55,000 cases. In 1928, Barbey's pack remained at 55,000 but fell drastically in 1929 to 25,341 for two reasons: the Sand Island seining grounds had virtually been destroyed by the new channel which cut the island in two, and because for some reason, that year had been the poorest fishing season on the Columbia River since 1922. The *Morning Astorian* on August 27, 1929, said, "Seining operations of the Barbey Packing Company on Sand Island were abandoned yesterday. Catches had been small of late, the return not meeting the overhead."

Nevertheless, the Barbey Packing Company thrived during those five years and by 1930, it had emerged as one of the three top salmon packers on the Columbia River. In 1930, however, things had changed in the United States. The Depression was on and it would take every ounce of Henry Barbey's business acumen and his salmon packing skills to weather the next ten years. He was up to it, however, and 1940 found the Barbey Packing Co. in good shape and ready to face the war years which were just around the corner.

The Mayday *tied up at the east end of the Barbey Packing Corp.*
dock at Astoria.

Chapter 11

BARBEY MOVES HIS SALMON
CANNERY TO ASTORIA

It was no secret that Henry Barbey was planning to expand his salmon packing operation after the 1927 salmon season. Instead of traveling south to California for the winter as had been his custom, he had remained at his Seaside home, making frequent trips to Astoria. He had been seen at Uppertown, looking at the site of what had once been the huge Hammond Lumber Co. plant. Fire had destroyed the mill in 1922 and it had not been rebuilt. The site had docks, railroad sidings, and a good deep water basin but it did not suit Henry Barbey's needs and he began to look elsewhere for a cannery site.

Henry Barbey's affairs were beginning to be of considerable interest to influential Astorians. The Barbey Packing Co. had come a long way from its small beginning back in 1910 and indeed was now recognized as one of the major salmon packing firms of the area.

After Barbey won the Sand Island leases in 1925, he began to be watched and commented upon by the *Astorian Budget*, Astoria's leading newspaper. Frequent articles appeared concerning Barbey's activities but instead of being referred to as a "small independent salmon packer", Barbey was now labeled as "the largest seine operator on the Columbia River", and as "one of the largest cold storage operators on the river."

There was good reason for this new respect. The *Budget* in February of 1928, said, "During the 1927 season, the Barbey Packing Co. put up 208 tierces containing 166,400 pounds of mild cured salmon together with 57,000 pounds of frozen steelhead. Barbey's canned salmon pack during 1927 amounted to 41,333 full cases, being one of the largest on the Columbia River."

The Barbey Packing Co. at Flavel.

Barbey's sudden purchase of the Allen & Hendrickson canning plant at Rainier, Oregon, in April of 1927 as well as his lease of the Chris Schmidt cold storage plant in 1926 had made it obvious that Henry Barbey was expanding. It was also obvious that his next move would be to bring his salmon packing operations into Astoria because of the advantages that town had over Flavel.

During the winter of 1927, it was reported that Barbey had purchased a tract of land of about fifty acres of waterfront property at the mouth of the Skipanon river, near his Flavel cannery. This rumor gave rise to a belief that he was planning to put up a new cannery and cold storage facility on that site.

Henry Barbey, as usual, kept what he was doing to himself. He was the sole owner and operator of the Barbey Packing Co. and answered to no one. He had no stockholders or partners to report to and was able to move ahead whenever he wanted with whatever plans he himself devised.

On February 17, 1928 it was announced that Henry Barbey had purchased a tract of waterfront property just east of the Port of Astoria terminals from the Sanborn-Cutting Company, long time salmon packers. The first reports stated that Barbey would erect a big, modern cold storage plant together with net racks, canned salmon warehouses, and storage for seine equipment on the site but a few days later, Henry Barbey let a contract with Henry Makela and Son to build a modern, combined salmon cannery and cold storage plant on the site.

Barbey's move was a decided triumph for the commissioners of the Port of Astoria. In 1927, they had been searching for new sources of business for the Port and, hearing that Barbey was looking for a possible salmon packing plant site, did everything they could to persuade Barbey to locate his plant adjacent to the Port of Astoria property. Graham Barbey in later years said, "They were so anxious to have my father there that they offered him 99 years of free office space at Pier 1 for his operations, and many other incentives to locate there but my father never did take them up on that offer. He thought it might obligate him to the Port of Astoria sometime in the future."

It is easy to understand why R.R. Bartlett, then manager of the Port, and the Port commissioners were anxious to persuade new industries to locate on the property. The Port depended on the shipping lines such as the Luckenbach Steamship Co. and the Panama Pacific Steamship Co. to dock there to discharge and pick up cargoes. Canned salmon then was carried through the Panama Canal to the New York markets and each time a ship docked at the Port, the Port made money from docking charges, and were also able to give longshoremen working at the Port of Astoria more work time.

The site at the Port did have enough good points in favor of it to make it easy for Henry Barbey to go ahead on the deal. Railroad sidings ran up into the Port property near the Pillsbury mill which could be used for shipping salmon out by rail and for bringing in cans and other supplies and equipment to the cannery. The northern edge of the Port docks ran east and west, adjacent to the river's ship channel and, by joining the new cannery buildings to that dock, Barbey would have ample deep water frontage on the river for unloading boats, and for shipping out freight.

There was a road leading out from Taylor Avenue to the dock's edge which could be used by his workers to get to and from work, and also by trucks hauling freight and other

A barge load of salmon at the Barbey Packing Co. in 1950, the last year the seining grounds operated. (Photo courtesy Columbia River Maritime Museum).

supplies to the cannery. As it turned out, Henry Barbey had to do considerable work on this roadway through the years to keep it useable for his trucks and men.

The plans called for two big buildings to be built upon pilings over the water with one side 100 feet long facing the Columbia River. One building housed the salmon cannery and the other was a two-story warehouse. A loading dock would be located on the east end, also facing on deep water. An office area with two apartments above was located to the south of these buildings while cold storage facilities and other needed work and storage areas made up the rest of the building.

The apartments built over the office were not designed for the Barbey family to use but rather were for two long-time employees. One of the two apartments was used by Rhoda Ross, who was Henry Barbey's secretary and bookkeeper, and the other was for Will Ellis, who had been with Barbey for many years at Flavel. Ellis was responsible for firing the cannery boilers and kept such early and late hours at this job that Barbey thought he should be housed at the plant. Will Ellis had a wife and a six year old daughter

The Barbey Packing Co. warehouse on Portway St. in Astoria, built in 1940. This was where the canned salmon was loaded on rail cars for New York. To the left is the corner of the Chinese bunkhouse. (Photo courtesy Columbia River Maritime Museum.)

Bonnie Jean. They lived in the apartment until he retired many years later.

The cold storage facility was a modernly equipped plant with two ice machines, one of twenty-ton and one of five-ton capacity, together with complete sharp and cold rooms for the storage of frozen and mild cured fish, as well as for their preparation.

In addition to the big cannery buildings, Henry Barbey also built a Chinese bunkhouse south of the cannery on the shore just north of Taylor Avenue where there was room for the Chinese crew to put in their inevitable vegetable garden. The bunkhouse was first built on pilings over the water but was moved to solid ground later after the Chinese protested about the lack of garden space.

While the new buildings were being built, Barbey and his crew were busy dismantling the cannery at Flavel. All useable equipment and supplies had to be packed and moved into the new plant as soon as possible so that everything would be ready when the first salmon of the 1928 fishing season arrived at the new cannery.

He also removed all of his equipment and supplies from the Chris Schmidt cold storage plant which he had been leasing, and moved all of it into the new building. This was done later in the season simply because the new cold storage plant could not be completed in time to be used for that season.

Barbey's Chinese crew and many of his regular staff of cannery employees were kept on the payroll through those early spring months of 1928 to move the supplies and equipment from the Hill Terminals to Astoria, and to help set up the new plant. Apparently, the work was completed on time and the new Barbey Packing Co. cannery at the Port of Astoria was in business during that salmon canning season of 1928 because the *Astorian Budget* reported in August of that year that the Barbey Packing Co. had put up a 60,000 case pack as well as 300 tierces of mild cure salmon. This pack was second to the CRPA's pack of 115,000 cases and was 10,000 more cases than Union Fish's pack of 50,000. Total pack for the Columbia River that year was 446,000 cases.

The following year, however, the situation was different and by the end of that 1929 season, the *Astorian Budget* reported, "The Columbia River season as a whole was the poorest since 1922. More salmon brought in from along the coast, and less from the river which shows that fishing is declining here."

Back then, even spring fishing seasons could be poor. Clarence Sigurdson of Warrenton, who was working for Barbey on his Pillar Rock seining grounds, said, "I think the second year I was there we started the first of May fishing and we caught hardly any fish — practically nothing — and this went on for about a week, I think, and down came a letter from Henry Barbey to Chesley Smith, telling him to close down the grounds and pay off the crew until the first of June."

"There was a P.S. on that letter, however. It said, 'I just happened to think that if the crew wanted to fish anyway, I would be willing to let them have free use of the grounds, the seines, the boats and horses, and they pay the expenses of the boats and the horses and the cookhouse and the cooks. I'll give them gillnet prices on the fish they catch and they can use the grounds free.' "

Chesley Smith, long-time seining ground foreman. Photo courtesy Robert Smith, Reedsport, Oregon.

Clarence Sigurdson went on with his story: "There were some of them out there on the seining grounds who said that if Barbey can't make it, why should we try? One said, "Oh, no, to heck with him. If he don't want to pay us, we'll just quit and then he can look for somebody else to run his grounds when the fish start running."

Clarence then spoke up and said, "Now, wait a minute. I've had a little experience in this fish business. The way the fish act sometimes, there's practically no fish but pretty soon they all start running at once — a big run of them. Supposing there is no fish for awhile and then the latter part of May a run comes in, we can knock them dead for awhile.

I'm willing to take a chance on that happening."

"Well, we got to talking it over and we all took a vote and decided to stay and fish for ourselves. The boys also demanded that when Chesley Smith made the agreement with Barbey, he was to insist that no matter how good the fishing was, the crew would stay on shares until the first of June. "Make sure he understands that", they said.

Barbey's note of agreement came back the following day. To it, he added, "The deal is okay but it just so happens that the first of June is on a Saturday so we'll make it the third of June."

Clarence chuckled as he looked back to a time sixty years ago. "So the crew stayed and we started fishing on our own, and it was kind of exciting at that. Every day when the fish were weighed, everyone would gather around to find out how many fish they got. They would get out their paper and pencils and figure out prices, costs, expenses and so forth.

"The first few days we were getting only about two or three dollars a day apiece but it kept getting better and better and I think our biggest day was along on the tail end there when we made about twenty dollars apiece. The understanding was that everyone got the same except for Chesley Smith who got extra because he was the foreman.

"We had some unexpected expenses, however. We lost a skiff — someone had left it with its nose up on the beach and forgot to tie it up — and the tide came in and the skiff was lost. I spent some time going all over the river, trying to find that skiff. Well, old Barbey charged us $85 for that skiff and some of the guys were squawking about that but I pointed out to them that we were the ones who lost it so we should be the ones who paid for it. We also bought a big barrel of cylinder oil which made some of them complain, saying that we hadn't used a barrel of oil, but the bill came in then and there were some things we had used that were left over so it all came out about even.

"Barbey lived up to his word and we wound up averaging about $8.33 a day apiece which was about double what we usually got. That came out to about $190. a month which

Henry Barbey and son Graham at
the Seaside beach house in 1925.

was not bad at all and Barbey got his fish and kept the cannery open. In June, we went back to the old system."

The spring and summer of 1929 were not the best of times for Henry Barbey. Fishing was down and that was the year when the Indians hit Sand Island, cutting down the fishing there. In spite of a reduced pack, however, Henry Barbey kept his Barbey Packing Co. moving and was ready in 1930 to try again. The stock market crash of 1929 had not affected him in any way since he owned no stock. Every cent of his money was invested in his own salmon packing company so he was not dependent in any way on stock investments.

During the years he had operated his cannery at Flavel, Henry Barbey had commuted from his Seaside home each day during the operating season. A house on Avenue I became available for rent after the owner, Randolph Flagg, decided to open a dress shop on East Broadway in Portland. Barbey took a long lease on this house and the Barbey family lived there until they moved into Astoria following the construction of the new Barbey Packing Co. at the Port of Astoria, a move made necessary by the additional distance Henry Barbey would have to drive each day. Graham Barbey recalled later, "The twice-daily drive to Flavel from Seaside was bad enough in those days of poor roads and unreliable automobiles, but when my father found that he would have to drive an additional hour each day, it was too much. We moved to Astoria."

Henry Barbey was still driving his sporty Stutz Bearcat in 1930 but he was always in the market for a new car. He loved big heavy powerful automobiles and when a Cadillac dealer in Portland phoned to tell him that they had a 16 cylinder Cadillac coupe they would like to sell him, he decided to trade in the Stutz so he took his son Graham and drove to Portland to pick up the new car.

"The dealership, Clark Cadillac, was located at 21st and Burnside," Graham later recalled, "and was on a slight slope. Unfortunately, the Stutz had air brakes and the air container had a hole in it so we had no brakes. My father was traveling down Burnside and was going to turn into the lower door of the building where they had the used car department. He was unable to turn in because he was going too fast and had no way to slow the car down. As I recall, we went around that block several times before we slowed down enough to pass through that door safely."

Graham chuckled as he recalled the rest of the story. "About a month after that, my father received a long distance phone call from some man who had bought the Stutz. He was calling from the Portland jail because he had gotten a parking ticket and when the police checked the records, they found that there were eight or ten speeding tickets out against the Stutz which my father had amassed and neglected to take care of. The man calling wanted my father to come up and bail him out but Henry Barbey told him that he had the wrong number and hung up."

Driving anywhere in those days was an adventure, according to Graham Barbey. "I can recall in 1922, we drove to Portland in my father's Packard touring car. It had isinglass windows that snapped on in case of rain. The roads were poor and full of chuckholes so we carried two spare tires, one behind the other, hung on the back of the car. I remember that the Packard caught fire on that trip but my father grabbed a lap robe and put it out.

"We stayed at the Weinhard-Astoria Hotel in Astoria the first night and then drove on up to Rainier to spend the second night there at the Rainier Hotel. That was about as far as a car could travel then in one day of hard driving. I remember at breakfast the next morning, we read in the newspaper that Astoria had burned the previous night and the Weinhard Hotel had burned to the ground so we had gotten out just in time."

The Astoria Fire of December 1922, which completely destroyed the famous Weinhard-Astoria Hotel, was confined to the downtown section and did not come anywhere near most of the salmon packing plants in the city so that particular industry was not affected by the disaster. Barbey, of course, was still operating his salmon cannery at Flavel in 1922.

Many of the stories about Henry Barbey center about him and the automobiles he drove. "One time much later on," Graham recalled, "we were living at the Astoria Hotel. That must have been right after my father built the Astoria cannery because we had to move to Astoria to be closer to his work. We had four rooms at the hotel, two bedrooms, two baths, and a living room. We ate out at restaurants on Commercial street, mostly at one place my mother called 'the greasy spoon' ".

One weekend, my parents invited the Jack Latourettes from Portland to be their guests. They played bridge in the evening and one time when my father was the dummy, he suggested to Jack that he should park his car over in the Gallant Garage where he kept his cars because the police gave any car parked on Astoria streets overnight a ticket. He said that he would go out and put Jack's car away for him while he was dummy.

"He took me with him," Graham said, "and we found the

Henry Barbey practicing his golf swing in front of the Barbey Seaside beach house in 1925.

car and drove it over to the garage but when my father tried to put on the hand brake, or the emergency brake as they called it in those days, he couldn't find it so he had to coast the car up against the garage wall to hold it there. When we returned to the hotel suite, my father asked Jack where his hand brake was. Mrs. Latourette then piped up and said, 'Oh, Jack, I forgot to tell you. It came off in my hand the other day so I put it into a paper bag and put it on the back seat.' "

Henry Barbey took up golf when he lived at Seaside, thinking that the recreation and the exercise would be good for him. He dressed the part in golf knickers and argyle socks as was customary in those days. His golfing partners included W.L. Thompson of CRPA, Bob Bartlett of the Port of Astoria, Bill Trembley who owned the Trembley sawmill at Warrenton, W.P. O'Brien of the Clatsop mill, and Bart Claghorn who came to Astoria about that time to manage Union Fish.

During those early days, the Barbey family lived in the Seaside home during the salmon-packing months and then would lease an apartment in Portland for November, December, and January at the Sovereign Hotel on Broadway or the Ambassador Apartments on Sixth Avenue. As has been mentioned before, the family moved to California during the remainder of each winter, returning again to Seaside in April.

When asked about his schooling, Graham Barbey said that he had bounced around quite a bit at different schools during those years. "I went to Seaside grade school while we were living at Seaside but transferred to Ladd school during our Portland months. I went a half year to Lewis and Clark school, now Central school, in Astoria but when we were in California, I attended the Wilton Place grade school. I also attended Astoria high school during either my sophomore or junior year."

"Finally, I became tired of moving from school to school so my parents sent me to Menlo school which is south of San Francisco near the Stanford campus. I went there for three years. After I graduated from that school, I attended Stanford University and graduated from there in 1941."

"It was an interesting life during those early days in Seaside", Graham Barbey remarked once, looking back over the years. "My father worked long hours and we had difficulty at times knowing when we could expect him."

*Henry Barbey on board a company
cannery tender in 1922.*

"This led to some funny incidents in our Seaside life. We had neighbors named Barde who had a maid named Grace. We also had a maid and her name was also Grace. Our phone numbers were also very similar. One evening, my father arrived home and found that we had already eaten. He was quite annoyed and asked why we hadn't waited for him before eating dinner. 'I called and told Grace that I would be coming,' he said.

"We called Grace in and asked her why she had not relayed my father's message but she looked puzzled and said that she had not talked to my father at all that day. It turned out that my father must have called the neighbor's house and talked with their maid. My father suddenly realized that our poor neighbors were probably patiently waiting for their father to arrive home from Portland for dinner after their maid Grace had told them he would be coming."

Henry Barbey's move to Astoria changed the Barbey family's entire life style, forcing them to adopt new living patterns to fit the new environment and conditions. The 1930s turned out to be ten years of change in the salmon packing industry and saw the sudden introduction of the albacore tuna packing industry into the area. Henry Barbey had to use every ounce of his good business judgment and ability to weather those years but the Barbey Packing Co. emerged into the 1940s intact and holding a secure spot as one of the leaders of the salmon and albacore tuna packing industry on the Columbia river.

Chapter 12

BUEY WONG AND
THE CHINESE CREW

"I think if there was one key man at the Barbey Packing Co. besides Mr. Barbey, it was Buey Wong."

Mrs. Dorothy Caughey Johnson, former tuna cleaner and office worker at the Barbey plant in the 1940s, made that statement recently at her home at Tacoma. "Buey ran the Chinese crew and kept his eyes on other parts of the operations. Everyone knew him and liked him. Graham Barbey was in the army at that time and was gone most of the time so Buey was always there to help out."

Jue Bue Wong, better known as Buey, had been with Henry Barbey since the days when Barbey was operating his Portland fish operation, and the two men worked together off and on for the next forty years at Portland, Flavel and Astoria.

When Henry Barbey took over the Pillar Rock Packing Co. for the fall run of 1912, he also inherited the crew of the cannery. The Chinese foreman there was Hu Sing. Later, his son Eugene Sing Kwan was a Chinese foreman for Barbey at his Astoria packing plant while Buey was absent on a long-awaited trip to China.

Henry Barbey, like most of the other salmon packers, depended heavily upon Chinese workers for the processing of the raw salmon. Like the other cannery owners, he had to use a Chinese contractor to secure the laborers, feed and house them, and keep them on the job throughout the canning season.

Chinese workers first appeared in Astoria in 1872 when George Hume, one of the early salmon canners, brought in the first crews to help process the salmon. Before this time, the packers had used regular laborers but these had proven too unreliable for the fast-paced work of the salmon season. A full and experienced crew of men was essential to a salmon packer if he was to take full advantage of the salmon runs. When the salmon came in, they had to be processed immediately. There was no middle ground.

By 1880, according to the Clatsop County census, there were more than two thousand Chinese living in the county and almost all of these were cannery workers. As the years passed, some Chinese left cannery work for truck gardening, cooking, and other jobs available to them in the town. There was also a solid core of Chinese merchants in Astoria, all congregated near the intersection of 6th and Bond Streets, who catered to the other Chinese with Chinese foods, clothing, medical supplies, fireworks, and all the other items used by them in maintaining their Chinese ways. The Chinese workers in many ways adapted to the American way of doing things while at the same time keeping certain aspects of their natural cultural life intact.

A contracting system soon developed in the town. A salmon packer would not hire individual workers but would arrange with a Chinese contractor to furnish him so many men for the year's pack. The contractor was responsible for getting the men, housing them, feeding them, and paying their wages. In return, the canneryman would pay the contractor a lump sum each year, out of which the Chinese contractor paid his expenses and pocketed the rest as his profit.

The system worked well and relieved the packer of one of his biggest headaches when the salmon were running. Would he have a full and reliable crew available for work at that time? The contracting system guaranteed him that he would. Since the same Chinese gang returned to the cannery each year, a continuity was established. Henry Barbey knew that he would have good efficient workers for his canning season, and the Chinese knew that they would have a good steady job, a comfortable place to live, and an income which, while not lavish, was average for the times.

There were many Chinese contracting firms operating in the Pacific Northwest and each Columbia River packing company had its favorite. CRPA, for example, used the contracting firm of Dogg & Lam for all of its various canning enterprises including those in Alaska. A statement from 1918 shows that they submitted a total billing at the end of that year amounting to more than $130,000. The statement is broken down into wages paid by the hour to the Chinese workmen for doing various jobs. For example, labeling was billed at 6 cents a case while strapping was 3½ cents. The men of the crew received $369 apiece for that season's work based on a total billing of 60 cents a case.

Henry Barbey's yearly figure for Chinese labor varied but records show he was paying about $10,000 a year during the 1930s. When Buey was doing the Barbey contracting, he received a dollar a case for all fish packed. Out of this, he provided all of the necessities for the Chinese crew except for the bunkhouse which Henry Barbey provided. In Astoria, the bunkhouse was located south of the cannery by the railroad tracks which ran parallel to Taylor Avenue and which was about a five-minute walk from the cannery.

A contract with a cannery could be a lucrative proposition for whichever Chinese had that contract. Graham Barbey can recall Buey giving his father a fancy Christmas gift such as a set of golf clubs each year. "But then," he said, "the unions came in and that ended the Chinese contracting system. The foreman got more money in salary than the people working for him but he was no longer able to get the extras that came with the contracting system. A smart frugal Chinese man could make a great deal of money contracting for a cannery."

Contrary to many published reports, the Chinese cannery workers lived in relative comfort in the bunkhouse. Each man had his own room although they all ate together in a common dining hall. A bathroom was shared by all and, as one of the workers put it, "It was first come, first served."

Dorothy Caughey Johnson said, "I was at the bunkhouse many times. It was very bare in there. There were no personal possessions, no pictures on the wall, and no flowers on the table.

"Helen Ho Yee was the cook there and she had a giant cement stove which had big steel pans called woks. There were two of them. There was a second room that had a table and chairs and benches, and down the hall were the individual rooms. Outside was their garden — they loved their greens.

"I used to go up there when we were working overtime — there were no restaurants nearby, you know. Helen would invite me up there to eat with the crew who went to the bunkhouse to eat each of their meals. They often had plain rice with some kind of greens they raised in their garden. I don't know what it was but it tasted different than the food in a Chinese restaurant. They liked peanut butter and watermelon. They ate fish — the tomcod would run each year and they would dry them, I think."

Graham Barbey later confirmed this. "The Chinese foreman would drop a net through the dock and they would catch carp and they would hang those fish up like clothes on a clothesline to dry. Any money the foreman could save on that kind of thing, he was able to pocket".

Other Barbey employees were invited to the Chinese bunkhouse to eat with them at times. Esther Rinne, at one time Barbey's floor lady in the salmon section, said, "I ate there for about three months one time. Helen would say to me, 'You come and eat with us', and I would say, 'Do you have a spoon?' and she would laugh. They always had to have a spoon for me because they ate with those chopsticks."

Jim Ferguson, a former production manager at Barbeys who now lives in Seattle, remembers Helen very well. "She used to bring me these things wrapped in bamboo leaves with rice and nuts and raisins in them. Delicious!"

Besides the carp, tomcod and other scrap fish the Chinese were able to catch through or off the end of the dock using nets or handlines, parts of other fish were also used for eating. In the old days before such scrap became valuable, they got salmon cheeks and bellies from the cannery butchering section and used these. When they could get sturgeon, they would remove the backbone and cut it up for soup. Actually, it was a big, long bundle of nerves rather than bone and it was removed by cutting a hole in the tail end of the sturgeon and then pulling the grey slippery bundle of cords out by hand.

At one time, Buey returned to China and Eugene Sing took over as foreman but then Buey returned and regained his old job. Later, Buey developed cancer and had to quit work and once again Eugene Sing became the foreman.

The Chinese workers did not have many expenses and saving money for the eventual return to their ancestral home in China was a ritual with them. Many of them built up a considerable sum of money in working toward that goal. Hop Sing, known as Hoppy, died in Astoria and more than $15,000 was found sewed up in his sports jacket.

Buey finally achieved the ambition of most of the Chinese cannery workers living in Astoria. He saved his money and eventually was able to return to his native home in China to live. He converted the money into gold and hid it in the walls of his home there, but misfortune hit him, and he had to come back to Astoria and to the Barbey Packing Co. again, an experience which gave him a lasting hatred of Communism.

"Communists?" he would say. "I'll tell you about the goddamn Communists. Goddamn thieves, that's what they are. I work all my life and save my money and then go home again to live in peace. I hid my money in the walls of my house but the Communists heard about it and came to my house and told me that I would have to share my money with my neighbors if I was to be a good Communist but I wouldn't do that so they took it all, goddamn them."

Buey was fond of telling about his big family back in China and one time Jim Ferguson asked him how he could have so many children there when he had spent so many years in Astoria. Eugene Sing, who was listening, laughed and said, "Oh, he's got good neighbors."

Whenever old-time Barbey employees get together, sooner or later someone will come up with his favorite Buey story.

Mrs. Esther Rinne said, "When Buey came back from China, I worked with him and he taught me how to grade fish and that sort of thing. He sure was a good partner. I really liked him. When I quit to go over to Bumble Bee (CRPA), Buey got so mad he threw cans all over, but I didn't like it at Bumble Bee because they were so jealous of newcomers so I worked one day and the next day I was standing behind the counter in Barbey's office when Buey came in, all smiles. "I told you that you wouldn't like it over there," he said.

Mrs. Rinne laughed as she remembered another memorable Buey moment. "We used to open the two big sliding doors that led out to the dock, during the summer weather, and there were always some men out there, loafing around or fishing on the dock and some of them would occasionally wander through the cannery. We caught one of them once in the ladies room going through the coats. Another time, one of them was fooling around up where the fish were butchered and came back after awhile with his coat all buttoned up, but below the coat we could see the big tail of a fresh salmon hanging out. Buey got so mad! He went up to him, grabbed the salmon out from under his coat and screamed in that funny way he had. "Watsa matta with you, goddamn thief. Gimme that salmon and get the hell out of here." Buey was holding that big fish — it must have weighed forty pounds — and he looked like he was going to hit the poor man with it but the thief got out of the cannery fast and that was that."

Dorothy Caughey Johnson remembers during the war years when Barbey had a government contract and federal inspectors were around the place constantly. They prohibited smoking near the fish and poor Buey, who was an inveterate smoker, walked around glumly dangling an unlighted cigarette from his mouth, muttering about the "goddamn government regulations and inspectors."

One time, Buey somehow got locked inside one of the cold storage rooms and was unable to get out for about six hours. When someone finally opened the door, poor Buey came out shivering and muttering to himself about "the goddamn cold storage doors".

Kee Brown, a well-known Astoria Chinese, was another of the Barbey foremen. He first worked for New England Fish Co. and came to Barbeys to supervise the operation at the time when Barbey was canning crab and salmon for them under their Pillar Rock label. A story about Kee Brown always caused a chuckle at the Barbey office. When Kee Brown wanted his son to come to the United States, Graham

Barbey signed a paper to assist him. When the son arrived, he turned out to be 55 years old. The relationships of the Chinese to one another always was confusing to the average American.

The Chinese also confused the Social Security people. Buey had one man who came every year with the crew but each year he changed his name, thus creating a first-class headache for government officials later on.

Certainly, the Chinese crews were indispensible to Henry Barbey. They remembered him as a very good boss, a kind man who was always solicitous of their welfare. At times, he would stroll down to the Chinese bunkhouse to see "the boys" and to talk with them. Even Henry Barbey was careful in his relationships with them, knowing that they followed the orders of the foreman, so all instructions to them went through the foreman. That was the way it was and everyone respected that custom.

Graham Barbey was aware of this problem in communications. "My father couldn't speak any Chinese but our Chinese foreman and all of the workers could. My father would talk to one of the workers and if the poor Chinaman couldn't understand, my father would just talk louder. The worker didn't understand what the boss wanted but he knew he wanted something so he ran and got the foreman and solved the problem that way."

Usually, the Chinese crew at the Barbey Packing Co. numbered about twenty-four. Their primary job was to butcher the salmon as they arrived at the cannery. The fish would be unloaded from the seining scow, purse seiner, or from a gillnet boat, and would be put into big two-wheeled carts and delivered to the butchering room.

Salmon arriving from the fisheries near The Dalles came by railroad refrigerator cars and would be sided near the Pillsbury flour mill west of the cannery. The Chinese would unload the car there and then bring the salmon into the cannery using the two-wheeled fish carts.

After the salmon were butchered and scaled, each salmon was graded according to color and specie. Only the finest salmon rated a No. 1 label. The different grades were put into different carts and kept separate all the way through the canning process so that the No. 1 fish always ended up in No. 1 cans. The public always got what they paid for from Henry Barbey.

The Chinamen (as they were called in those days) stood at a long table, each at a separate station. They were clad in knee boots with long yellow oilcloth aprons. As the carts were wheeled in, a boy would gaff the salmon and toss them up onto the table where the Chinese butchers grasped them by the tails, gutted them, removed the heads and tails, and then shoved them through the hole in front of them to the slimers on the other side of the table who finished cleaning and washing the fish inside and out. The cleaned carcasses were then sent to a machine which cut them into slices designed to fit into cans. The entrails, heads, and other discarded parts were shoved through another hole in the table and disappeared into the fast-moving murky waters of the Columbia River far below. This practice is not allowed today because of laws protecting the quality of the river.

The writer can vividly remember an occasion in about 1942 when he was working for the Barbey Packing Co. and was given the job of supplying the Chinese butchers with salmon. "I gaffed each salmon in the head and then tossed it onto the table to be butchered by the waiting Chinese. I was not too good at the job and one time, in my enthusiasm, I tossed a big salmon a bit too far. It skidded across the table and disappeared into the hole, ending up in the river below. The old Chinese butcher stopped work, stared at the hole for a moment, looked at me, sighed, and went back to work again. Luckily for me, no one ever mentioned the incident to either Henry or Graham Barbey."

All of the experienced cannerymen knew that none of the discarded parts of the salmon ever reached the shoreline but disappeared within seconds into the hungry mouths of millions of suckers, carp and other fish which made their homes in the river under the cannery floors. The moment discarded fish parts hit the water, there was a foaming swirl as hundreds of fish fought for the parts, and any that escaped the fishes' mouths were soon picked up by the thousands of circling seagulls which made their homes near the canneries. The presence of these fish and birds made the disposal of these parts of the salmon complete.

In later years, many of these salmon parts were saved and made into fish food for the hatcheries. Packed into ten-pound boxes they sold for 15¢ a pound. The parts would be fast-frozen first and then picked up later by the Oregon Fish Commission trucks to be taken to the hatchery.

One of the best parts of the salmon and one virtually unknown to the general public were the salmon cheeks. There was one of these dollar sized pieces of flesh on each side of the salmon's head. In the early days, the Chinese would cut these out and would sell them, eat them, or would give them away to their friends. The cheeks sold for about a dollar a dozen which was a good source of extra revenue for the Chinese crew. Other good parts saved included the tails and the belly flesh, both discarded during the process of preparing the salmon for packing. At first the eggs were discarded in the Columbia River with the heads, tails and entrails. Later they were frozen and sold to the fish hatcheries. Finally, the Japanese sent technicians to the canneries to salt and freeze them and pack them in wooden boxes for shipment to Japan.

The Chinese workers ate salmon eggs as a delicacy but later on, the Japanese heard of these eggs and bought all they could get, using it as cavier although they had another name for it. According to Graham Barbey, the eggs brought what was considered a very fancy price, better than $1.40 a pound in the 1970s.

Eventually, it was found that there was some value in salmon oil so the heads, tails, and entrails were ground up and the salmon oil added to the cans to enhance the quality and flavor of the canned salmon.

Each Chinese butcher had his own set of knives which he allowed no one else to touch. These were kept razor keen and were carefully cleaned and oiled each night to ensure their sharpness. "They were our bread and butter," Henry Young, a former cannery worker said.

When the butchering was finished for the day, the Chinese crew would be put on other jobs. There was always labeling to be done, and the empty cans had to be taken to the loft for use later. In the early days of the salmon packing industry, the Chinese made the cans by hand with solder, tin snips, and pieces of tin, but after the mechanical can maker was invented, this art became a lost one.

A feature of all the canneries was the hot coffee available. As one Chinese put it, they had to have the coffee to keep warm. After the canneries were unionized, regular coffee breaks were set at 10 a.m. and 3 p.m. and big boxes of pastries were provided by the owners. These were always served in one part of the cannery, usually identified by the rows of private cups hanging from nails on the walls. It must be added here that the hot coffee and pastries served twice daily were also provided to the women salmon packers and women tuna cleaners and packers, most of whom were either Finnish or Norwegian. They did not need the coffee to warm them but enjoyed the coffee break as it is an old Scandinavian custom and is a very social gathering for them. It would be a foolish salmon packer who would dare try to eliminate those pastries and coffee. His crews would have soon departed for other more congenial surroundings where Astoria customs are observed without fail.

Dorothy Caughey Johnson said, "I used to order the pastries for the coffee breaks from the Home Bakery. In the winter time, someone would go up and pick up the ten dozen or so we used but they delivered them in the summer when we used more. We had twenty-four Chinese, twenty-four salmon packers, ten dock and warehouse workers, and one hundred in the tuna cannery plus the office force so we used a lot of them. I used to fix the coffee too."

"Henry Barbey would occasionally come out and have a coffee break and the ladies loved that. He would talk to them and they enjoyed that immensely. He always wore grey suits and was a very nice looking man."

Butchering was a cold job. The salmon canneries were built with wooden floors with big cracks between the boards. These were there so the floor could be hosed down and cleaned more easily. Those cracks also caused cold drafts to sweep up from the cold river below. This and the open doors leading out to the docks kept the inside temperature of the butcher room even with the prevailing outside temperature. It was a cold, bone-wracking job and it is a wonder that all of the Chinese workers did not come down with pneumonia each year.

During the days when the salmon were running and work went on in the cannery for eighteen or twenty hours a day, there was no leisure time for the typical Chinese worker, but once the season was over or the salmon run had slackened, they had more time. As one said, "Occasionally we would get a Sunday off and then we might walk into town to have some fun. It is only about a two mile walk from the Barbey bunkhouse to 6th and Bond where the Chinese section of Astoria was located so it didn't take us long to make the trip."

"What did we do there? Well, generally we would do a bit of shopping and then go and watch some gambling or games. There was lots of gambling in the Chinese section of town in those days. Once in a while we would go up to Portland but that was very seldom."

Even though the canning season lasted for a limited time, there was usually work for those who wanted to stay during the off-season. They could live in the bunkhouse free of charge although they had to do their own cooking. The bunkhouse was warm and comfortable and was the only home in this country that many of the men had.

Generally, Astorians liked the Chinese. They early learned that the men were quiet and peaceful, even though their customs were foreign to the early-day Astorians. Their love of gambling irritated many a lawman who did his best to close down the gambling dens, usually without success. The ever-lasting firecrackers did annoy many early Astorians such as D.C. Ireland, founder of the *Tri-Weekly Astorian* in 1873, who complained that to live next door to a Chinese washhouse was like living in a war zone because of the constant popping of the firecrackers.

Many of the Chinese found homes among the Astorians. Some left the canneries and took jobs in the houses of many prominent Astorians as cooks or as a yardman. Some of them moved to the outskirts of town and raised vegetables which they sold around town to the busy housewives and to grocery stores. At one time, the sight of a Chinese truck farmer carrying a double load of vegetables on his shoulders was a common sight in the town.

The Howe family lived in Astor Court on Denver Avenue across from what is now Tapiola Park. The writer can remember as a small boy walking past the Howe place on his way down to the wreck of the *T.J. Potter* for a swim and seeing Mr. Howe working in his garden with short rubber boots, and a kind of round conical hat. His garden was laid out neatly in long rows, each raised perfectly about six inches above the ground. It was a beautiful sight to see. Today, that garden is covered with brush and alder trees and there is no sign of the Howe gardens which were there once."

Other Chinese went into business, selling primarily to other Chinese. For many years, the Lum Quing grocery on Bond Street was one of the most colorful businesses in the city. There were Chinese washhouses, stores, restaurants, and even Chinese doctors who seemed to specialize in herbal medicine.

The most remarkable thing about the Chinese community in the early days was the almost complete absence of women, the result of early-day national immigration and hiring policies. Almost all of the men who were hired to work in the canneries were single men, although there were always some with wives and families back in China. Through the years, a few of them managed to get their wives into the United States and within a few years Chinese women would be seen in the Chinese section and even on the streets. Then Chinese children began appearing at the local schools. It was a gradual process, but by 1910 there was a stable Chinese population living in Astoria.

In late years, various writers have decried the treatment of the Chinese by the whites in Astoria but local residents and Chinese alike know that this is not the way it was. Astoria has always been a cosmopolitan community simply because of its nature as a seaport. Members of foreign races were familiar sights in the city as they still are today. True, the

Chinese were more numerous than the other minorities, but by their nature, they fit in because of their traits of hard work, cleanliness, and a regard for the family and for education.

Even though there were numerous arrests of the Chinese by the authorities for gambling, there were no violent racial episodes ever recorded in the city. True, a tong war hit the town during the 1920s and several Chinese men were killed but the trouble was brought to Astoria by out-of-town Chinese. Indeed, local Chinese at the time asked the local police for protection from the tong warfare.

Today, there are few Chinese living in Astoria or in the lower Columbia area. As the canneries closed one by one, the Chinese crews left for other places and other jobs. There are still a few Chinese living and working in the town but they have become almost totally Americanized and seem to have forgotten or else to have put aside the colorful customs of the old-time Chinese residents and no longer add to the color and the glamour of what was once a colorful and glamorous town.

Chapter 13

CHIEF CHARLEY INVADES
SAND ISLAND

Never in his wildest dreams did Henry Barbey imagine that he would have to fight off an Indian raid to hold his seining rights on Sand Island but this is exactly what he had to do in 1929 when Chief Big Charley and sixty-five of his Indian braves from the Shoalwater tribe suddenly appeared on the Washington side of the Columbia River and invaded the fishing grounds of the white men, determined to test the tribe's rights to fish where and when they pleased.

Chief George A. Charley was the son of Light House Charley Ma-tote, who received his appointment as head chief of the Shoalwater Bay tribe on August 10, 1876. He was the last of the old time chiefs but after he drowned in the river, Chief Charley took over the leadership of the tribe, dropping the name "Ma-tote". According to a news story which appeared in the *Morning Astorian* at that time, the Indians were from the Quinalt Indian reservation.

William L. Thompson of the CRPA and his seining crew on Peacock Spit had to bear the brunt of the first attack by the irate Indians. During the early morning hours of July 18, 1929, Big Charley and his braves descended upon the Spit in boats and scows looking for fish rather than scalps. They crept in, fished one tide, loaded their equipment back into the boats and departed before the seining crews were awake and could do anything to stop the sudden invasion of their seining ground.

In 1928, the Indians had filed suit in federal court at Tacoma contending that under a treaty signed in 1855 at the time they ceded their tribal lands to the government, they retained

Chief George A. Charlie of the Shoalwater Tribe with his wife and four of his children. (Photo courtesy Ilwaco Heritage Center.)

the right to fish along with the white men in their "usual and accustomed places". However, this suit had not come to trial at that time so there was no way of knowing which way the final decision would go.

CRPA's answer to the Indians' contention was that at the time the treaty was signed, Peacock Spit, as it now existed, had not been formed and would not be formed until many years later following construction of the North Jetty at the mouth of the Columbia River. If this was the case, the Spit was not a "usual and accustomed place" which the Indians used for fishing.

The wheels of justice, however, grind slowly and nothing had been decided. The salmon run never moved slowly and neither did the tides. Seining grounds operated when the salmon were running and when the fishing tides were right. Because of these facts, CRPA was determined to go ahead and protect its seining rights in any way it could.

In the case of the Shoalwater Bay tribe, the statement of CRPA was absolutely correct. These Indians had never fished along the Columbia River in the days before the white men dominated the river. James G. Swan, one of the first white settlers in the Southwest Washington area, said in his book,

The Northwest Coast, that the Quinault Indians fished with weirs as well as with spears and hooks in the Quinault River, catching a species of small salmon similar to the Chinook salmon but never attaining its larger size. The Quinalts were catching bluebacks which are similar to the Puget Sound sockeyes. The dominant tribe on the Washington side of the river at that time was the Chinook Indians who lived in the area running along the river from Point Ellice to Point Chinook, a flat land bordered by a sandy beach. The Chinooks fished along the shore there using nets much like those used later at the white men's seining grounds. Salmon was so plentiful in those early days that there was no need for them to fish anywhere else. Sand Island was there then but the Indians did not fish there because there was no reason to paddle out in their canoes to use that fishing ground when they could catch all the salmon they wanted right on their own beach in front of their own village.

Henry Barbey was familiar with the history of the Indians' claims to fishing rights and he knew that, regardless of the logic or legality of them, the Quinaults were there in force and would probably hit Sand Island as they had Peacock Spit. He knew that they were claiming Sand Island as a "usual and accustomed place for fishing" too and he also knew that it was simply a matter of time before the Quinaults appeared at his leased ground.

There was a legal difference in the two seining ground leases, however. Over on Peacock Spit, CRPA was leasing that seining ground from the State of Washington under the name of the Bakers Bay Fish Co., a subsidiary of the giant packing concern, but over on Sand Island, Henry Barbey had a lease from the federal government under his own name. William L. Thompson and CRPA could only invoke Washington law in defending his seining ground rights but Henry Barbey could call in the formidable power of the federal government to help maintain his lease on the Sand Island seining grounds. He could also call in State of Oregon fish officials because Sand Island did lay within Oregon's state boundaries and was therefore subject to Oregon's fishing laws.

Thompson knew that the Indians would only strike when the seining tides were good and the next one would be at 3 p.m. that afternoon. With trouble imminent, he called in his seining crews and bosses and laid out a strategy designed to repel the Indian invaders and yet keep the threat of violence to a minimum.

Promptly at three that afternoon, W.L. Thompson, a formidable and impressive figure with a cigar clenched in his mouth, perched on top of the watchtower on the sands, sighted the enemy flotilla approaching the Spit. There were boats and scows loaded with horses and nets and, according to CRPA officials, towed by a power boat owned by P.J. McGowan & Sons, a Washington packing company which had been engaged in a court battle with CRPA over fishing rights on Peacock Spit.

It was a sizeable armada but tough old W.L. Thompson refused to be daunted. He called out his reserve army which consisted of about eighty college boys who were spending their summer vacation working on the seining grounds to earn enough money to return to college in the fall. Arming each of the young men with a twelve-foot oar, Thompson sent his force out to do battle with the invading Indians.

He had picked the right men for the battle. The college boys were bored with pulling in nets day and night and had been itching for some excitement. Whooping with joy, the collegians seized their oars and dashed into the surf to meet the incoming Indians. As fast as the Indian boats touched the sand, they were pushed off and out into the current by Thompson's boys. And back on the sands, the other members of the seining crew waited, applauding each good move by the collegiate band.

Thompson had ordered the boys to refrain from breaking any heads or causing any bloodshed but it soon became apparent that both the Indians and the collegiates were beginning to lose their tempers and would soon be going beyond merely pushing the boats back and forth between the sand and the water.

It was an exciting and noisy scene. The boys were shouting college yells while the Indians were giving back a few war whoops of their own. The horses on the scows were milling about neighing with anxiety and the seining crews added to the noise with a few encouraging whoops, catcalls and good-humored obscenities.

Just when it seemed that real violence would break out, Deputy Sheriff Myers of Ilwaco arrived to bring law and order to the embattled sand spit. Thompson had the law on his side. He had a legal lease from the State of Washington and insisted that Sheriff Myers enforce the law and order the Indians off the Spit.

Eventually, after a lengthy argument about tribal rights versus lease rights, the Indians decided to leave peacefully. By this time, the tide had gone out and the Indian boats were stuck fast in the sands of Peacock Spit. Once more, the collegiates got out their oars and helpfully pushed the Indian boats out into the current. Peace once more came to the Spit but by this time the tide had changed and a good seining tide had been lost. Big Charley and his fellow tribesmen had lost the battle but Thompson and CRPA had lost a good tide and probably several thousand dollars worth of salmon so there were no real winners in that first skirmish.

In a newspaper interview the following day, W.L. Thompson said, "It looked serious for a time but ended in a laugh." He added that he did not expect further trouble but that a lookout would be kept at all times in the future to guard against further raids.

Henry Barbey was expecting trouble on Sand Island. He knew that the Indians had made their point and were done with Peacock Spit and would be heading his way to lay claim to his seining grounds. He marshalled his forces and got ready to repel the Indian invaders if they showed up. He also notified both the federal government and the Oregon State Fish Commission, alerting them to the threatened Indian attack. Since Sand Island lay within the State of Oregon boundaries, fishing there required an Oregon commercial fishing license which he knew the Indians did not have. Federal authorities could enforce the law on the seining ground but had no jurisdiction over fishing in Oregon waters. The Oregon officials could enforce the fishing regulations in Oregon waters

Seining at Sand Island.

but had no authority on Sand Island which was a government reserve. It was a complicated situation but Henry Barbey covered every contingency and then sat back and waited for the expected developments.

Big Charley and his sixty-five braves arrived at Sand Island promptly on time for the seining tide but made no efforts to fish or to interfere with the Barbey seining operations. Some of them sat in their boats anchored off the sands and watched the seiners, while other Indians landed and lolled peacefully on the warm sand. Occasionally, they gave a raspberry to Bill Smith, Oregon deputy fish warden of the Lower Columbia patrol, as he sailed back and forth along the Sand Island shores, watching the Indians to make sure they were not fishing but making no attempt to interfere with their sunbathing.

As time passed and the Indians became bored with simply sitting there, they organized baseball teams, marked out a diamond, and spent several hours playing ball. Many of the college boys, pulling in the heavy seining nets and pitching heavy salmon, cast envious eyes at the cavorting Indian braves and wished that Henry Barbey would give them time off for a good baseball game with Chief Charlie and his men.

Henry Barbey, however, was in no mood to let his seining crews off to play baseball. As long as the Indians made no attempt to fish, he did not interfere with their pleasures. His seining crews worked as usual, pulling in the seines loaded with salmon, and putting the seine out for another haul. Finally, the fishing tide was over and the seining crew put away their equipment for the day. They put the horses into the barns, tied the boats to their moorings, and quit work. The Indians left Sand Island in their flotillas and returned to Ilwaco. It had been a draw for that day.

Two days later, however, something did happen finally which ended the conflict. David Baker, Indian seine boss in charge of forty Indians, invaded the seining grounds and attempted to put an Indian seine in the river during the tide. Deputy Smith moved in and confiscated the Indians' big drag seine, skiff, and power launch, and arrested David Baker on a charge of commercial fishing in Oregon waters without a proper license. Baker was taken to Astoria where he posted $100 bail in justice court and was released. His confiscated gear, however, was held by the authorities.

Baker, a Taholah Indian leader, made no attempt to resist arrest and his followers immediately left Sand Island for Ilwaco although it was reported later that they had hauled in several tons of salmon during their operations on the island.

That was the end of the battle of the seining grounds for that year. The Indians had made their point and were heading for a court showdown on their tribal right versus the rights of the federal and state governments to lease the fishing places. Both Barbey and Thompson had made their points by defending their fishing leases which they felt had been obtained legally and therefore were binding on all. The Oregon Fish Commission had made its point about Indians or anyone else fishing in Oregon waters without a license.

Eventually, the affair came to court when the Indians asked for an injunction from Judge Neter of the federal court of Seattle, to keep CRPA's Baker Bay Fish Co. from operating on Peacock Spit. The suit was against CRPA but Barbey intervened in the case, even though he was seining only on Sand Island. As he said, "A decision in favor of the Indians may seriously affect seine and fish trap rights along the north shore of the Columbia River that are valued at several millions of dollars, and could affect the Barbey seining grounds on Sand Island." A.E. Clark, his attorney, was on hand to assist in the case.

The injunction was denied by the court and the Bakers Bay Fish Co. was allowed to continue seining operations on Peacock Spit. Strangely enough, the real winner in all of this was the Port of Ilwaco, a non-participant, because three-quarters of the rent derived by the State of Washington from the Peacock Spit lease went toward improving the port district facilities at Ilwaco, but there was no question that all of the salmon packing concerns including both the Barbey Packing Company and CRPA breathed easier after the court handed down its decision. Their seining rights not only on Peacock Spit but also on Sand Island and at other locations along the river were safe from Indian intrusions in the future.

Many years later, the Indians did get the rights to fish in their "usual and accustomed places" but by that time the seining grounds were gone, much of the salmon run had disappeared, and the impact of their rights was not nearly as serious as it would have been during the summer of 1929. The age-old controversy between the red men and the white men over fishing rights goes on, however, and as long as there are salmon still in the Columbia River, it will probably continue.

Many years later, Jim Ferguson, then production manager of the Barbey Packing Co., had a conversation with a government official about the controversial Boldt decision concerning Indian fishing rights. The official told him that inevitably the first group to lose its fishing privileges would be the commercial fishermen, then the sports fishermen, and the last ones fishing on the rivers would be the Indians.

He may have been right although all three groups still use the Columbia River. The disputes still go on, however, and perhaps it is inevitable that finally, the Indians will have all of the salmon fishing rights on the Columbia River as they did once very long ago.

Chapter 14

THE DEPRESSION DAYS

The early days of the Depression may have caused great havoc in other parts of the country but Astoria escaped much of the worst effects of those hectic years. The local lumber and logging interests suffered because of the shortage of money available for construction and building, but the fishing industry prospered because, as Graham Barbey said once, "In those days, a case of 48 one-pound tall cans of Columbia River salmon sold for as low as $10 for good quality salmon. A man could buy a case of salmon and a sack of potatoes and feed his family nourishing meals for what even at that point seemed a small amount of money."

When the stock market crashed in 1929, it did not affect Henry Barbey because he had all of his financial holdings invested in the Barbey Packing Company. Because of this, he was considered very financially successful at this time in contrast to many of his friends who had been in other types of businesses.

Graham Barbey said about this period of Henry Barbey's life, "I can recall my father leasing the Portland home on Westover Terrace from the owner of Vogan Candy Co. because business was tough for candy manufacturers and many others during those years. Many of them had to sell or rent their homes because they could not afford to keep them up.

"I can also recall a real estate salesman in Portland trying to sell my father the beautiful Ward Bowles home on Cumberland Road on Westover Terrace for $35,000. This house was a beautiful Italian style home complete with greenhouse and could easily be appraised today in Portland in excess of $600,000."

The Barbey home on Jerome avenue in Astoria, Oregon.

The Barbey family was still living at the Astoria Hotel during these days, but was looking for a permanent home in Astoria. After the Barbey Packing Company was built on the west end of Astoria in 1928, it was obvious that Henry Barbey and his family needed a permanent place to live in that city. They could have built a new residence, but Henry Barbey did not have the time nor the interest to supervise such a project, so they decided to buy a home that was already built.

Herb Palmberg, who now lives at Warrenton, said, "Henry Barbey bought my father's house on Jerome Avenue across from the Astoria High School in 1934. It was a very nice house but in those days the garage was in the back of the house. Barbey later changed that. He bought the lot next door and built a new three-car garage there on the west side of the house. I don't blame him. The old one was too hard to get into and to back out of. The Barbeys had big cars and they would never have gotten into the old garage because it had a tight curve around the back corner of the house.

"He also built the wall across the front of the property. We had big concrete urns — flower pots — out there once but he put the wall up, probably for protection and privacy, I guess, and got rid of the urns."

Henry and Ethel Barbey at home at their Astoria residence on Jerome avenue.

The big white house on Jerome avenue was built for Harry Hoefler, founder of the Hoefler Centennial Chocolates, who lived there for a few years before selling it to Charles Palmberg, well-known Astoria contractor who built many of Astoria's better buildings during the years he was in the contracting business. Strangely enough, he was also the builder of the Flavel Hotel where the Barbeys had lived back in 1919. Palmberg died in 1934 and his wife then sold the house to Henry Barbey.

Herb Palmberg, Charles's son, in speaking about the house, said, "It was a wonderful house. Upstairs, in the back, there was a kind of a library room with big open windows where you could look all over the river. We could go up there at night and see the hundreds of gillnet boats out on the river. It was a beautiful sight.

"As I recall, my mother sold the house to Henry Barbey for about $11,500. He was living down at the Astoria Hotel at the time. When he heard the house was for sale, he expressed an interest in it and subsequently bought it. I believe they lived there until he died."

Herb Palmberg was correct. The Barbey family moved into the Jerome Avenue house and lived there for the next thirty years. When the Henry Barbeys purchased the house they completely remodeled it over a two year period. They added two bathrooms, a breakfast room, a powder room, and the three-car garage. It was in this house that Henry Barbey died in 1964. During those thirty years, however, he kept busy at the cannery, meeting and coping with all of the changes brought by the Depression and World War II.

It has been mentioned that the changes in the physical structure of Sand Island forced Henry Barbey to make changes in the way he had to operate his seining grounds there. There was little that he could do during the term of his lease but that was up for renewal in 1930 and at that time, he set out on a new course.

Henry Barbey and W.L. Thompson of the CRPA, met during the early months of 1930 and devised a plan which would give the two salmon packing firms at least a fighting chance to seine on Sand Island. They decided to submit a joint bid for all of the five sites at a set figure much lower than the one Barbey had bid five years before. In addition, the two men agreed to seine on Peacock Spit and split the profits or losses on that seining ground as well.

Barbey and Thompson submitted a total joint bid of $45,175 per annum for all five Sand Island sites, or a total of $225,875 for the next five years. This bid was less than Barbey had bid by himself in 1925.

The bids for individual sites on a yearly basis were: Site No. 1 — $8595; Site No. 2 — $17,595; Site No. 3 — $12,695; Site No. 4 — $5,695; Site No. 5 — $595.

The only other bids submitted that day were by Point Adams Packing Co. which bid $4,550 for Site No. 4 and $150 for Site No. 5. Alex Muller bid $125 for Site No. 5.

The leases were approved by the government on March 30, 1930, giving Barbey and CRPA exclusive rights to Sand Island until 1935. At the same time, the lease on Peacock Spit was approved by the State of Washington so the two salmon packing companies now had full control of the two seining grounds closest to the mouth of the Columbia river.

*John and Julia Barbey in 1922 with children Dan, Caroline, Henry,
and Hazel. Grandson Graham is in foreground.*

In April, the Barbey Packing Co. applied for a federal
permit to construct a wharf which would extend out into
the Columbia River from the south side of Sand Island about
900 feet and would be located about one-half mile west of
the east end. He also applied for permission to erect four
traps behind the wharf.

The CRFPU immediately went on record as opposing the
issuance of such a permit to Barbey, complaining that such
a wharf would block out one of the best drifts on the lower
river. At this same meeting, the gillnetters also authorized their
officials to tell a state-wide organization of sportsmen that
they would have no objection to the introduction of an initiative
measure barring all fish traps in the Oregon waters of the
Columbia River, and that they would support such a measure.

On May 5, a preliminary examination of the trap sites on
Sand Island was made by M.T. Hoy, Master Fish Warden
of Oregon, and Fish Commissioners Chris Lienenweber and
Robert Farrell. In spite of the protests of the CRFPU, the
permits were granted and Barbey set to work building his
wharf and traps.

Using the new traps and his usual seines, Henry Barbey managed to have a good season in 1930 while W.L. Thompson over on Peacock Spit did about as well. It was a good year for fishing for the gillnetters as well as for the seiners and all groups looked forward to the completion of a successful spring and summer.

However, by the beginning of August, 1930, the salmon run had slackened off drastically for the gillnetters and it was not long until they began putting the blame on Barbey and on Thompson, claiming that the new docks and traps at both locations were hurting the gillnet fisheries.

As will be described in the chapter on the war with the gillnetters, many of these gillnetters took action against the seines by attempting to interfere with seining operations on both Sand Island and on Peacock Spit, beginning on August 4th. The trouble lasted only for about a week but echoes of that conflict sounded over the lower Columbia River for years afterwards.

Later in the month, reports of an initiative petition requesting the state legislature in 1931 to abolish all seines and traps in waters over which the State of Oregon had jurisdiction was noted by the *Astorian Budget*. Officials of the CRFPU told a reporter of that paper that the union had nothing to do with the matter and that the subject had never been brought up at a union meeting.

On August 26, however, a new legal move was made by a gillnetter named John Strandholm of Astoria who brought suit against Henry Barbey and the Oregon Fish Commission to remove the dock and fish traps Barbey had built on the south side of Sand Island, alleging that they interfered with his customary drifts in that area and interfered with navigation of those waters.

Henry Barbey suffered one of his rare defeats on this occasion because on November 27, 1931, a decision was handed down in the circuit court at Portland ordering the Barbey Packing Co. to tear up three fish traps on Sand Island and also to remove all parts of the disputed dock and roadway which extended beyond the ordinary high water line. This, of course, would destroy the dock making

The Sand Island seining grounds bunkhouse and cookhouse at low tide. (Photo courtesy Byron Fitzgerald, Salem, Oregon.)

it impossible for Barbey to use the *Mayday* or any other cannery tender in any fishing operations on Sand Island or in the adjoining fisheries. The decision also required the company to give up its licenses for the three traps sites and ordered the fish commission to cancel these licenses.

Unquestionably, this could have been a costly blow for Henry Barbey. He and Thompson still had the lease on the five sites on Sand Island and, with the help of the fish traps and the dock, had done well during the salmon fishing seasons of 1930 and 1931, but without those structures available for use, most of Sand Island would be rendered almost useless because of the changes in the island started in 1929 and continued each year thereafter.

Strangely enough, the physical changes in Sand Island were actually helping the west end of the island adjacent to the Peacock Spit seining grounds. The rivers channels were constantly changing and for three years the waters between Sand Island and Peacock Spit were being transformed so that seining operations could be carried on in places once considered completely unuseable by normal standards. Both Barbey and Thompson had noted these changes and decided to take advantage of them.

The first thing they did was to cancel their leases on Sand Island. It was announced on May 14, 1932, that the War Department had cancelled those leases. At the time, Barbey said, "There has been a mistaken report circulated that we asked for a reduction in the Sand Island lease prices. We did not. We asked for an outright cancellation of the leases and that is what we obtained. Changing conditions on the island have made it of little value as a fishing ground and, in view of other circumstances in the industry, is not a good proposition, and was an impossible one under the terms of the lease."

Since the lease for the seining sites had become effective on May 1, 1930, when they were cancelled, it appeared all property on the island had belonged to the Federal government since that time.

Under the terms of the Sand Island lease, Barbey and CRPA had 30 days in which to remove all physical property from the lease sites. If this was not done, the buildings, docks, traps and all other physical structures became the property of the U.S. government. Barbey and CRPA declined to remove anything on the island and allowed the dock and other structures to revert back to Federal ownership. In this odd situation, the decree of the state court was without force as effecting the interests of the United States since its interests could not be effected by decree of a court in a suit to which it is not a party. The commanding officer at Ft. Stevens was directed to permit no one to demolish, remove or interfere with the dock in question so, for all practical purposes, the State court decree in the Stranholm case was unenforceable.

Even though they could no longer seine on the five sites on Sand Island, Barbey and CRPA could still use the island and the structures on it in common with any other interested party so the disputed dock, roadway, and other structures were still used daily in spite of the state court decree.

Henry Barbey continued to fish on the island although now he had his crew fishing on what was called Peacock Spit Island, the new seining ground created by the currents of the river between the island and the mainland of Washington. He continued to use the buildings and other structures on the island but was not actually fishing off the island. By this adroit move, Barbey was able to get enough seining ground fish to operate that season for a good profit.

On July 9, 1932, the Barbey Packing Co. and CRPA filed suit in federal court to enjoin the government from prohibiting them from fishing on Sand Island. They claimed that the vacation order by the War Department endangered the whole Columbia River fishing industry.

Unofficially, the *Astorian Budget* reported, the buildings and equipment on the island were being used as a base for seining operations on Peacock Spit, which, of course, was leased from the State of Washington.

For the next few years, this issue of seining on Sand Island kept coming up in courts and in other places. Complicating the issue was the fact that Sand Island was at that time claimed by Oregon. Washington claimed Peacock Spit and ownership of the seining ground there was a disputed issue. At the same time, Oregon was trying to get the Federal Government to release all rights to the island. Finally, Washington was eliminated from the battle after outlawing in 1934 all pound nets, traps, fish wheels, set nets, or any fixed appliance in Washington waters.

Even so, in 1935, the state of Washington tried to force CRPA and the Barbey Packing Co. to refrain from using fish traps on Sand Island, claiming that they were illegal in the state and therefore could not be used in those waters off Sand Island. The two packing firms obtained an injunction from superior court which prevented the Washington State Fish Commission from interfering with these traps because they were in Oregon waters.

Later that same year, Judge Howard K. Zimmerman of the circuit court in Oregon put a temporary restraining order on H.J. Barbey of the Barbey Packing Co. from operating a seine under a license granted him by the Oregon Fish Commission to seine on Peacock Spit Island. One of the arguments presented in that case was that "there is no Peacock Spit Island for which the license was granted but that the site is a part of the river bed, and, or, an accretion to Sand Island."

This order was issued after a suit was filed against Barbey by Arne Johnson and five other gillnet fishermen. The suit's other grounds were that seining operations there interfered with the usual and accustomed operations as gillnetters on the old Republic and Peacock Spit drifts. If such a seine is operated, the operator will catch between twenty-five and thirty tons of fish per day, thus depriving other fishermen on the river of their "reasonable and expected share" of the fish entering the river.

Other plaintiffs with Johnson were E.A. Storvick, Victor Haglund, Ed Karvonen, Clyde Lieser, and Emil Eckholm.

On June 3, 1935, Henry Barbey and W.L. Thompson struck back by appearing before the State of Oregon Land Board and asked that the so-called Oregon Sands or Peacock Spit Island in front of Sand Island be leased to them for seining purposes. They were opposed at this hearing by the CRFPU which represented 1500 gillnetters, by the Union Fishermen's Cooperative Packing Co., and by the federal government which claimed that Sand Island, leased to the federal government in 1864 by the State of Oregon included the so-called new sands.

Jay Bowerman, a Portland attorney who represented Barbey and Thompson, claimed that the state had nothing to lose in leasing the fishing grounds to his clients. He said that they would be willing to defend the state's claim to Sand Island in the courts against the federal government. Frank Franciscovich and Rep. Walter Norblad Jr., both of Astoria, were the attorneys representing the CRFPU and Union Fish.

It was at this time that Arvid Mattson, secretary of the fishermen's union, said that the group would be filing an initiative petition to bar all traps and seines from the Columbia River as the State of Washington had already done.

Legal battles over Sand Island and adjacent sands continued in the various courts for years after this but the Barbey Packing Co. and CRPA continued to fish from Sand Island, almost to the time seines were declared illegal by the State of Oregon. The two men took advantage of the fact that the legal status of Sand Island was never clearly set forth. As long as the federal government, the State of Oregon, and the State of Washington claimed jurisdiction on either the island or the adjacent waters, any court decision could be challenged in other courts on various technicalities.

The legal battles continued but so did the seining operations of both the Barbey Packing Co. and CRPA. As long as the waters around Sand Island produced salmon, neither side would give in and so the fight went on.

Henry Barbey, of course, was still getting fish at his Pillar Rock seining grounds, from Welch's Sands, and from Rabbit Island up at The Dalles so he was always able to put up a sizeable pack each year, regardless of his problems with Sand Island.

The 1930s brought another problem to the salmon industry on the lower Columbia River which caused all of the various factions of the industry to form a solid front to fight the new menace. Salmon packers, gillnetters, seiners, and trollers all united to fight the erection of the dams on the Columbia River, beginning with the proposed construction of Bonneville Dam in 1933.

Actually, dam building on the rivers and streams of the Columbia River basin had been a problem for many years. Dams for irrigation and for power had been erected on many salmon-producing tributaries of the Columbia River and, because most of these did not include facilities for allowing the migrating salmon to pass them, these early dams had taken a large toll on some of the traditional salmon runs. Others had been built with provisions for the safe passage of upriver bound fish but none of them had given any thought to the problems of getting the tiny salmon heading downstream towards the sea.

None of these early dams, however, had caused the major impact on the fisheries which the construction of Bonneville Dam would bring. It was to have a sixty foot head, far higher than anything ever built on the river, and certainly would end forever the salmon runs on the Columbia River if it was built without fish ladders.

So many objections were raised from so many sources that the Corps of Engineers were forced to include fish passage facilities in their plans for the construction of the dam. Three were planned at different locations. One was on the Washington shore, one on Bradford Island, and the third on the Oregon side. All of them were combinations of a collecting trough leading into a series of stepped up pools, each about a foot higher than preceding one.

In addition to these ladders, the Corps of Engineers built four fish lifts which were combinations of an elevator and a ship's lock. The salmon enter the lock and were lifted to the top of the dam where they were released. As it turned out, the lifts were rarely used because of the effectiveness of the fish ladders.

Bypasses for the seabound fingerlings were built in three locations and were intended to deflect the tiny fish from entering the spillway or the turbines, and pass them safely by the dam.

The inclusion of all of these elements designed to help the salmon run survive the construction and operation of Bonneville Dam did not satisfy most members of the salmon fishing industry who consistently maintained that Bonneville should not be built because of its potentiality for destroying the salmon runs. They used every facility at their command but were unable to stop the construction of Bonneville. It was at their insistence, however, and that of others, that forced the government to face the fact that the salmon run had to be saved by the inclusion of ladders, lifts, and bypasses. It was the best that members of the fishing industry could do.

The first salmon run went through the Bonneville Dam barrier in the spring of 1938 and it was anxiously watched by not only the engineers and fish biologists, but by the salmon industry of the river, to see what effect if any the dam had on the run. More than a million fish went over the ladders in that first year and went on their way upstream to spawn. Many of the government people claimed that the dam had not harmed the salmon run at all but fishing interests pointed out that this was the first time the fish had been counted. There was no way to tell how many had gone past that point in previous years. The total effect of the dam on salmon runs has never been completely or satisfactorily determined by anyone, but the dam is an accomplished fact and cannot be changed now.

Certainly, construction of Bonneville Dam did effect the salmon fishing at that locality. It eliminated any fishwheels still operating there, some seining and gillnetting sites, and many Indian fishing places. These are all gone forever.

Subsequent construction of Grand Coulee far up the Columbia River was another matter. Its 310-foot height made it impossible to build any kind of device which would enable fish to pass this huge concrete barrier so this dam effectively cut off more than a thousand miles of salmon spawning grounds forever. Fishing interest fought against its construction but were unable to overcome the forces in favor of building the dam and finally had to bow to the inevitable loss of these future migrating salmon.

Through the years since that time, other dams such as McNary Dam and The Dalles Dam have been built on the Columbia River, each with its own series of ladders and bypasses. The salmon runs have continued in spite of these additional barriers but each has taken its toll and reduced the annual runs of salmon.

Henry Barbey continued to pack salmon despite all of the problems of the 1930s and put up good packs of salmon each year. The introduction of the albacore tuna in 1936 added a new dimension to the Columbia river packing industry and Barbey was one of the first salmon packers to enter this new industry. He met and mastered each challenge as it came up, and by the end of that hectic decade, was generally regarded as one of the giants of the industry.

Ethel Barbey in the living room of the Barbey residence in Astoria.

Chapter 15

AT WAR WITH
THE GILLNETTERS

No one really expected August 4, 1930 to be any different from any of the other days of that seining season. It was a bright, sunlit day with a warm sea breeze moving in from the bar to the west. The men of the Barbey Packing Co.'s seining crews had been laboring as usual with the seines, horses, boats, and the other gear which were needed to operate the seining ground in an efficient manner.

The salmon had been running well during that summer and the seining hauls had been big and profitable. The crews visualized bonuses and heavy paychecks while Henry Barbey looked forward to a profitable season under the new joint lease with CRPA for the Sand Island seining grounds.

Henry Barbey had gone out to Sand Island on that day for one of his occasional visits. He came not to direct but to observe. Barbey hired foremen to direct his varied operations and, as long as they did their work satisfactorily, he left them alone, but that is not to say that he was disinterested in what was going on. He always liked to have his fingers on the pulse of his enterprises.

He stood on the beach, idly watching several gillnet boats head towards Sand Island. Strange, he thought, that they would be out on a day like this. Conditions were wrong for gillnetting. Bright sunlight streaming into the water would expose their nets to the moving salmon which would avoid them by simply swimming away in the opposite direction.

Barbey counted eight gillnetters moving towards the area where the seines were usually put into the water. They waited until the seines were in and then cast from twenty-five to fifty fathoms of their nets out and started a drift just ahead of the seines, effectively driving away from the seines any salmon in the vicinity. Their move also slowed up the operations of the seines.

Henry Barbey watched angrily as the gillnetters hauled their nets in after the seine site had been crossed and then returned to the original location for another run across the seines. It was obvious that the gillnetters were barely pretending to fish. "Why, they are just trying to lead the salmon schools away from the seining grounds by splitting the schools," Barbey said furiously.

He did not know it but at that same time just to the west of them over on Peacock Spit, another group of gillnetters was operating in the same manner over the CRPA seines. Each time the seines were put out into the water, gillnetters moved in ahead of them, dragging the water with their nets, efficiently keeping the moving salmon out of the seines.

"Put the seine out again," W.L. Thompson said, and watched as his Peacock Spit crew began the laborious process of running a seine. As the seine went out, one of the gillnetters, Thompson later claimed, cut the headline with a hatchet. The drag on the tail line was pulling the horses into the water forcing the seine operators to cut the tail line. Thompson watched glumly as the net was carried out by a strong ebb tide. It disappeared but was later picked up off the south jetty in a damaged condition.

Meanwhile, back on Sand Island, Henry Barbey told his seine foreman to put the seine out again and watched as it went out with the gillnetters running ahead of it. In seining ground operations, the net with its lower edge held down under the water with weights and its top edge floating on the surface buoyed up by floats, was pulled out into the current by a small boat which made a huge circle in the water before pulling the end of the net back up to the beach. At that point teams of horses standing in the water would be hitched to the net and would then pull the seine back to the dry sands. As the seine came into the shallow waters, men tending the net would carefully guide it in, making sure salmon trapped in the net could not escape under or over it. The hauls in the seine could be enormous. The record apparently was made in 1921 when 60,000 pounds of salmon were netted in one seining haul.

This time, however, the seines were empty. The gillnetters had effectively moved the salmon away from the seines. "Put her out again," Barbey ordered. "If we can't catch any salmon, let's get some of those gillnetters." He watched as the net moved through the water in the usual huge circle. One of the gillnetters refused to move out of the way and was caught in the net and pulled towards the shore, dragging his gillnet behind. The horses and men caught the tail end of the line and hauled mightily, dragging the hapless gillnetter and his boat up on the sands. They left him there and went back for another run with the seine. Later in the day, the seining crews dragged the marooned gillnetter and his boat back into the water. They did the same for a few other gillnetters who had also been dragged in during the day.

Over on Peacock Spit, W.L. Thompson was having the same kind of problems and tried to solve them in the same manner by pulling gillnetters in as they were caught in the seines. The seiners lost the day's battle, however, because very few salmon were netted during the day and one day's catch lost was a major item during the height of the salmon run.

The following day, the situation was no better. Gillnetters congregated at both seining grounds, interfering with the operations of the seines and preventing the ground operators from catching any salmon. One gillnetter stated quite frankly that it was the intention of the gillnetters to drive the salmon away from the seining grounds in retaliation for the traps that CRPA built on Peacock Spit and for the dock that Barbey built on the south side of Sand Island, both of which, the gillnetters said, interfered with their fishing in those areas.

The license numbers of the offending gillnet boats had been taken down by the seining ground crews. Both Barbey and Thompson went to South Bend, Washington, and filed suits against fifty-three gillnetters, charging conspiracy, and seeking damages in large amounts, plus restraining orders banning

The boat loading dock on Sand Island. (Photo courtesy Byron Fitzgerald, Salem, Oregon.)

Seining at Sand Island.

the gillnetters designated from interfering with future seining operations on either Sand Island or Peacock Spit. These suits were filed in Washington because most of the fishermen named had Washington licenses. Peacock Spit also was under Washington jurisdiction.

In a statement backed by both Thompson and Barbey, Thompson said, "We do not question the right of the gillnetters to fish in these waters. We do not and have not ever objected to their fishing in a legitimate, orderly and usual manner but we intend to stand on our own rights, which we hold equal to theirs; to conduct our operations in an orderly manner and without interference. The fishermen involved in this dispute have not been actually fishing, and have not been going through the regular and orderly procedure of gillnet fishing.

"The operation of traps and seines is necessary for the stability of the river industry. In low water years the gillnetters cannot take the fish and the canners must get them from fixed gear. In high water years, the fixed gear cannot take the fish and the gillnetters get them.

"There are two-hundred men earning a living on these seining grounds and continued interference with this source would throw them out of a job.

"We are ready to give every consideration to any gillnetter legitimately engaged in his usual pursuits but we demand fair treatment in return."

Henry Barbey got deputy sheriffs Tony Christensen and E.G. Willikson to go with him out to the seining grounds to serve more restraining orders on gillnetters charged with interfering with seining operations. Nine papers were served although Christensen said that some of the fishermen served appeared to be extremely bitter and tossed papers handed to them into the river without examining their contents.

The following day, Henry Barbey gave an interview to an *Astorian Budget* reporter to give his side of the affair. He rarely talked with newspapermen but in this case, he felt that his message would reach the rank and file of gillnetters if it came from a familiar newspaper.

"Gillnetters," he said, "are simply prejudicing the minds of the public for their type of gear by their present action of sabotage and refusal to obey court orders.

"The large majority of gillnetters are law abiding, self respecting citizens, but among this group is an irresponsible radical element that has no respect for our courts or for the law of this country in which they live. Witness a court injunction receiving no attention from a gillnetter, the same gillnetter continuing malicious interference after a restraining order is issued. Witness a sheriff serving a court paper and a gillnetter casting the paper into the river without reading it as though the courts of this land mean nothing to him.

"On one hand, the class of gillnetter I speak of cut an expensive seine and let it drift into the ocean without the least assistance at rescue. Another gillnetter cuts the bridle of a seine full of salmon, destroys the haul and necessitates the picking up of the seine in the river.

"On the other hand are the seiners; two hundred or more; mostly college lads working on Sand Island and Peacock Spit earning their money, in a good many instances, to complete courses. If a boat is anchored maliciously and wilfully they bring it in when making their haul and the boat is unharmed and towed to safety. The gillnetter wishes to force these young men out of employment. The law gives these young men the right to seine. The gillnetters disregard this law. He takes this law into his own hands."

Henry Barbey must have had a presentiment about things to come when he said, "There will come a time when the gillnetters might wish to seek favors from the public and they should go with clean hands. These same self-respecting law-abiding gillnetters should wake up and see how certain radical elements are wrecking their cause. Gillnetters wish to abolish seines and traps. Every seine and trap that is now operating in the Columbia River is lawful fishing gear and is necessary to stabilize the industry."

Henry Barbey lived to see the gillnetters seek public favor by setting up an organization called Salmon For All, Inc., an Astoria-based, non-profit organization which led the fight to defeat a ballot measure in 1964 which would have banned all gillnetting on the lower Columbia River. Then, it was the gillnetters trying to fight off efforts by sports fishing groups to force them off the river instead of the seiners trying to fight off efforts by the gillnetters to force them off the river. Henry Barbey must have marveled to see the changes the years brought in the fortunes of individuals and groups.

A few days after this, Superior Judge H.W.H. Jewen of Pacific County, Washington, made permanent an injunction obtained by the Bakers Bay Fish Co., a subsidiary of the CRPA, to prevent a group of fifty-three gillnetters from interfering with seining on Peacock Spit, which effectively ended the 1930 war between the seiners and the gillnetters. There was still another suit pending in Oregon on the troubles at Sand Island but both sides recognized now that the fight was over — at least for the year.

Another suit, however, was filed a few days later by a William Lampa and twelve other defendants asking $5,000 for direct damage done his boat and nets and for general damages in the sum of $5,000 from the Barbey Packing Co. and CRPA. In this complaint, the gillnetters stated that their nets were damaged and boats injured by the seining ground crew while they were engaged in pursuing their usual occupation of fishing off Sand Island on August 4. These were the gillnetters whose boats were hauled out of the waters by the seiners on that day.

Ordinarily, legal maneuvers by both sides in such a question would have put the entire matter on hold but in this case, the packing companies could not wait for the matter to be settled by the courts. The salmon were running now and each day that went by without the seines in the water was another day lost of the fishing season and thousands of dollars in revenue lost. It was imperative for both Barbey and Thompson to settle the matter temporarily so they could get back to their seining operations.

O.A. Wirkkala, superintendent of the CRPA operation at Ilwaco, was sent to confer with the Ilwaco, Washington gillnetters who were the fishermen involved in the interference of the seining at Peacock Spit and Sand Island. He found that the gillnetters wanted traps on Peacock Spit, and a dock and fish traps on Sand Island removed, claiming that these structures interfered with the gillnetters fishing operations in those areas.

In a gesture of conciliation, Thompson ordered the piles pulled from a fishtrap projecting from the southeast side of Peacock Spit but both he and Barbey refused to do anything about the disputed structures on Sand Island. As they pointed out, legal permits for the erection of these had been obtained and they were therefore legal. They also said that they were needed for a profitable operation of the Sand Island seining grounds.

Thompson said he ordered the trap on the Spit removed because even though it did not interfere with the fishing operations of the gillnetters, it could cause a fifteen or twenty minute delay to fishermen returning home to Ilwaco on half tide.

"We have no desire to interfere with or cause trouble for the fishermen and are having this trap removed," he said later.

"As to the Sand Island dock, the shoaling of the channels on the north side of the island has made it impossible to handle fish from that side. The dock is extended to a point where ten feet of water is available at mean low tide, the least depth feasible for running our tenders in and taking out a load."

Thompson went on and explained that the Oregon Fish Commission had made an extended investigation before they granted the trap licenses and had indicated that on ordinary drifts the gillnets did not come within 1,000 feet of the end of the dock or of the traps.

However, in interviews the following day, the gillnetters declared that the Peacock Spit trap which had been removed had seriously interfered with their fishing operations, and that the new Sand Island dock and adjacent traps not only blocked former gillnet drifts but were a menace to fishermen operating out from the island because they changed the current and it then carried the nets towards them.

Some of the gillnetters said that they had often "scratched" the island with their nets drifting over the spot where the dock and traps were located, and had found it a profitable fishing ground. It was reported that they believed that the establishment of traps along the island by the docks was but the beginning of plans to line the entire island with traps, subsequently destroying one of the best gillnetter grounds on the river.

"Once they get a foothold with the traps," one fisherman declared, "they get another site nearby and point out that no one could drift there anyway because it is too close to the other traps. Then they get one further ahead and so on until they have the sands lined with them, fishing twenty-four-hours a day, the cheapest way of fishing, and certain to land the biggest runs of salmon in the river."

It was a widely held belief that seine fish were cheaper than gillnet caught fish, and trap fish were the cheapest of all.

A fleet of several hundred gillnet boats milled around the seining grounds while seining was in progress on the morning of August 8 but there was little interference at that time with the seining crews. The war had reached a kind of stalemate simply because the tidal conditions were not good for seining and the approach of the weekend kept the gillnetters from making any long-range plans to cripple the seining grounds. There was some talk about the movement continuing after the weekend but, as it turned out, the worst of the gillnetter-seiner war of 1930 was over.

On August 13, 1930, the court at South Bend, Washington, sustained a request of CRPA's subsidiary, the Bakers Bay Fish Co., for restraining orders banning the gillnet fishermen from "maliciously interfering with the operation of the company's seines at Peacock Spit."

At the same time, the court ordered the Bakers Bay Fish Co. to refrain from interfering in any way with gillnetters engaged in fishing on the Columbia river in their "usual and accustomed manner".

While all of this legal maneuvering was going on, the spawning ground salmon continued to move up the river, past the seining grounds and past the gillnets, paying no attention at all to the controversy between the gillnetters and the seiners so an uneasy truce took place between the two groups. The salmon had to be taken at once or they would move on up the river and be lost forever to both the gillnetters and the seiners. Fish first and argue later became the watchword on the river and so the fight was dropped for the rest of that fishing season of 1930.

A few months later, Henry Barbey was able to look back on that salmon season of 1930 with some satisfaction. Even with the gillnetter trouble on Sand Island, his Astoria salmon cannery had put up a pack second only to CRPA's. Prices on canned salmon were down but, on the other hand, so were prices on labor and materials so it all worked out for the best.

He closed up his cannery that winter with a light heart. With all of its problems, 1930 had been a good year for him and for the Barbey Packing Co. Who could ask for more than that?

Chapter 16

THE PILLAR ROCK SANDS

"Now when you are out there weighing those fish at Pillar Rock Sands, there's only one person you're working for and that is me. You're not working for anyone else."

Clarence Sigurdson of Seaside recalled those words of Henry Barbey years later while reminiscing about the days he spent working for the Barbey Packing Company back in the early 1930s. Barbey had hired Clarence, then a very young man, to act as weighman at his seining grounds at Pillar Rock near the north side of the Columbia River and had taken him aside to give him his instructions before the fishing season opened.

Barbey went on. "Weigh those fish accurately, right down to the pound. I want to know exactly how many pounds of salmon that seining grounds is netting each day. And you bring those figures to me."

Clarence chuckled. "I soon found out why old Barbey was so insistent on this point. Out at Pillar Rock, they were more casual about the weight of the fish caught. When I got there, Chesley Smith, who was the foreman there at that time, told me that on the seining grounds, they never weighed them right out to the pound. 'If there's 195 pounds, we just call it 200 pounds. Same with 205 pounds. Round off the numbers. They're easier to keep track of.' "

"I found out why they did this later on," Clarence said. "Smith was on a percentage basis. He got a regular salary plus a bonus on poundage. A cent a pound, I think it was, so he liked to turn in round numbers. Needless to say, I followed the big boss' orders and weighed the salmon out to the exact pound."

Ernest C. Woodfield, seining ground foreman, at the Barbey Packing Co. Pillar Rock seining ground in 1937. (Photo courtesy Columbia River Maritime Museum).

Pillar Rock Sands tail boat named Graybar *after Graham Barbey. (Photo courtesy of Robert Smith, Reedsport, Oregon.)*

In his constant search for new sources of freshly-caught salmon, Henry Barbey had leased the Pillar Rock seining grounds in the early 1930s. Everding & Farrell had sold their Pillar Rock properties to New England Fish Co. in 1930, and Barbey had leased the seining ground from the new owners, and operated it for many years after that.

To handle Pillar Rock, Sand Island, and the other seining grounds he leased through the years, Henry Barbey depended upon a number of seining grounds foremen to run the operations there. Such famous foremen as Chesley Smith, Ernie Woodfield and his son Ernie Jr., and Brick Miller were some of the men he used for this position as has been mentioned before.

In those days, the seining grounds foremen were almost legendary characters: men of strong will and a great knowledge of men and the salmon, who were able to handle the crews out on the river and bring in catches pleasing to the owners. Such men as Henry Pice of Jim Crow Sands, Roscoe Miles of Kaboth Sands, George Kruckman of Desdemona Sands, and Ken Parker of Van Dusen Sands were all top hands, and often moved from sands to sands as the fishing industry changed. Of these men, the names Chesley Smith and Ernie Woodfield have come down through the years as epitomizing the very best in a field that always demanded top performance at all times and under all conditions.

Since these men moved from seining grounds to seining ground, it is difficult to place them with any kind of accuracy at one place during any one time but certainly Chesley Smith was the foreman at Sand Island during the early days of the Barbey Astoria operation and was the boss running the Pillar Rock Sands while Sigurdson was there, while by that time Ernie Woodfield had taken over at Sand Island.

Clarence Sigurdson picked up his story after describing his first meeting with Henry Barbey. "He took me out into the cannery and pointed out a boat tucked into one corner. 'That boat in the cannery there,' he said, 'You see the superintendent for it. Get the battery and the magneto, stuff like that on her, fill it up with gas, check her all out and when you are ready, tell him and he'll run it out for you on the hoist and set it into the water. When everything is set, take her up to Pillar Rock and tell Chesley that you are the new weighmaster.' "

"The boat Barbey pointed out to me was an old upriver gillnetter about twenty-six feet long but it looked fine to me so I set to work, trying to get it into shape."

While Clarence was working on the boat, his brother George Sigurdson, who was captain of the head launch *Juneta* at the time, came by and looked at the old boat. "What are you going to do with that?" he asked.

"I'm fixing it up to take up to the Pillar Rock seining ground," Clarence said. "I'm the new weighmaster there."

George walked around the boat slowly, looking it over. "That boat has a number on it and it should have a name. You figure out a name, rustle me up some paint and I'll put the name on it for you. Every boat should have a name."

"That sounded fine to me. George had studied show card writing when he went to OSC and he knew how to make a sign so I sat down and tried to think of a good name for my boat."

"Barbey's best label at that time was Barbey's Supreme and I thought that would be a pretty good name but then I thought of Sea Hag which also sounded good. When George came back later and asked me if I had thought of a name, I told him about the two I had thought of. He liked Sea Hag so I rustled him up a brush and some paint from the superintendent and George painted that name in letters four inches high on both sides of the boat and also on the bow. It really looked fine when he was done."

Later, while Clarence was working on the boat, he saw Henry Barbey approaching. "He came out of his office, walking in that funny way he had with his hands clasped in back of him and his head down as if he was thinking. He walked right by me and as far as I could see, never even glanced at the *Sea Hag* but when he got out to where the superintendent was standing on the dock, I could hear him say, 'Before that boat goes into the water, get that name off it. That boat is not supposed to go by name, it's registered by number — a state number.' "

"That was all he said and then he walked off but the superintendent came back to where I was and he was mad. He says, 'Boy, you got me in dutch now. I got you the paint and a brush to use and old man Barbey told me to get that name off of there.' He stomped off and came back with some more paint the same color as the boat was and I painted the names out but from that day on everybody, for years and years after that, called that boat the *Sea Hag*."

That was the way Henry Barbey ran things. He went everywhere and saw everything, even though it looked as if he weren't paying attention to anything. Occasionally, he would pause, place his glasses on his nose for a moment to look closely at something and then would take them off again and walk away holding the glasses in his hands again. Obviously, he needed the glasses for reading but was rarely seen with them on. Whether he was sensitive about wearing them or whether he just didn't like to bother with them was never known. He rarely said anything to anyone. If there was something wrong, he would tell a foreman or the superintendent and he would come and find out what was going on while Henry Barbey wandered on, looking at something else. He practiced a "hands off" kind of management and it worked fine for him.

After Sigurdson got his boat into shape, he headed out for the Pillar Rock Sands, located about sixteen miles upstream on the north side of the river, but Clarence had to follow the boat channels and they wandered about quite a bit so the trip actually measured about twenty miles.

The Pillar Rock Sands was located about a half-mile off Pillar Rock on the north channel and consisted of about two acres of land above high tide mark. There wasn't much there to look at, just a bunk house, a cookhouse and dining hall, and a few other outbuildings. It all looked temporary and jerry built and it was. Conditions out on the sands in the Columbia River changed so often and sometimes so violently and quickly that it was foolish to make permanent improvements at any time because no one knew how long they would last. The next storm or flood tide could sweep it all away and it would all have to be redone.

*Henry Barbey on board a cannery
tender in 1923.*

Riphath Christensen, who first went out to Pillar Rock in 1940, said, "The barn they used on Pillar Rock Sands was an old barge. The cook shack where we ate — that was up on pilings and we had two or three women as cooks. They lived there — stayed right there and they fed good. Excellent food."

"We had six teams there and they went up on the barge on a ramp. No spares at all. I don't remember us ever having a spare team. Two of those teams were on the tail end of the net and then on the head. They had four teams. We would go downstream and put the nets in. There was a small boat on the tail end of the seine and the net was on the barge. The boatman would go way out and make a big circle and then bring the rope in and hook it to the horses. We never hung the net up. It just stayed on the barge. They had a hook on the rope and it was hooked to the doubletrees on the horse.

Riphath Christensen went on with his description of seining on Pillar Rock Sands. "We had four teams on the head. There were always three teams pulling. When we got to the beach, we unhooked and then waded out into the water and gave the seine rope to another man who would hook it up again. They just kept on going around and around — I don't remember how many times. We always got salmon in that seine. I cannot ever remember finding any other kind of fish in there.

"There were six teamsters, probably two on the tail and four on the heads, all handling the horses, and then there were others on the boats and seines, maybe twenty-five men.

"We went down to Barbey's cannery to get hired for seining ground work," Riphath said. "When they were ready for us to go out there to start seining, we all gathered on the dock at Barbeys and rode the *Mayday* over to the grounds. We came in each weekend and I can remember one time I missed the boat so I ran over to CRPA and got it there. The *Mayday* stopped there to pick up men too."

Liquor was never much of a problem at the seining grounds. Foreman such as Chesley Smith absolutely prohibited drinking there and dismissal was the penalty for disobeying this order so all of drinking was done by the men in Astoria on weekends. Some of the men catching the boats at the beginning of each week would be somewhat the worse for wear and still showing effects of alcohol but each of these was provided with a life preserver and there is no record of any of them ever being lost in the river during the trip from Astoria to the seining grounds.

"My job out there on the Pillar Rock Sands was simple enough," Clarence Sigurdson said later. "I was in charge of weighing the salmon caught in the seines, and it was all done on the fish scow. There was a box on the scow about the size of two or three fish boxes and the bottom of it had a slope to it with a door on the side of the box. This big box was put on one side of a beam scale and weights were put on the other side. You put fish in the box until it was filled and then put weights on the other side until they both balanced. Each time, I wrote out a slip with the exact weight on it and then the fish were dumped into the scow for shipment back to the cannery."

"One time," Clarence said, "I was weighing the fish and one of them caught that day was the biggest salmon I had ever seen. It hit the scales at eighty-four pounds. Chesley Smith came along then and he said, 'That's the biggest salmon I have ever seen and I've been on the seining grounds all of my life.' So when the *Mayday*, Barbey's fish tender, arrived to pick up the fish scow, Chesley took this big fish over to the captain and told him to take the big salmon in to Mr. Barbey. It was special."

"When the *Mayday* got to the cannery dock, the captain called the superintendent over and said to him, 'Here's the biggest salmon we've ever seen, special for Mr. Barbey. It weighs eighty-four pounds.' Well, the superintendent put the big salmon into the refrigeration room and left it there for a couple of days. He thought that Barbey had special plans for the big fish so he just left it there, but finally he went out to the front office and said, "Say, what do you want me to do with that big fish?"

Barbey looked up, puzzled. "What big fish?"

"That eighty-four-pound Chinook we have on ice."

"What do you mean, what do we do with it?"

"Well," the superintendent said, "They said you wanted it. It's an eighty-four-pound salmon!"

Barbey just stared at him for a moment and then said, "What do I want with an eighty-four-pound salmon. Can it."

"But it's an eighty-four-pound Chinook salmon!"

"Can it," Barbey repeated. It was obvious to the superintendent that the old man was not impressed by any fish, no matter how big it was. Salmon was good for one thing as far as he was concerned and that was for canning purposes.

It should be mentioned here that while there have been

many tales of one hundred-pound salmon being caught in the Columbia River during the early days, none of these incidents can be verified. For the record, the largest Chinook salmon caught by an individual, weighed and verified, was caught by Capt. H.P. Nelson on May 29, 1914, who turned in an eighty-seven-pound Chinook salmon to Phil McConough at the Megler station. It was then turned over to S. Schmidt & Co. which had made a standing offer of $50 to be paid for the largest salmon caught that season. It was said that the big fish was to be exhibited at the 1915 fair at San Francisco but it is not known whether the salmon ever got there or not.

Strangely enough, another Columbia river eighty-seven-pound Chinook salmon appeared at the American Legion convention of 1931 held in Detroit, Michigan. Mike Cosovich, past commander of Clatsop Post 12, the Astoria delegate to the convention, took the big salmon to the convention but did not say who caught it. It was said that the five-feet, eight-inch long salmon was the main attraction there but there is no record as to what happened to this big fish. Presumably, hungry Legionaires ate it after the convention adjourned.

Olof Peterson, an Astoria gillnetter, caught an eighty-five-pound Chinook on July 13, 1907, which probably was the third largest salmon ever caught.

If legends can be believed, old Chief Tostum of the Clatsop Indian tribe, had the honor of catching the largest Chinook salmon back in the 1860s. According to John Nolan, an old-time resident of Astoria who told the story back in 1914, Chief Tostum was walking along the beach near what is today Hammond, Oregon, when he happened to see a big salmon wallowing around in a hole in the tide flats. He got a big stick and pulled the salmon out with that and was pulling it toward dry land when Capt. George Flavel happened to arrive on the scene. Seeing the huge fish, he offered the chief a five-dollar gold piece for his catch. Since the market price for salmon at that time was 15 cents apiece, Chief Tostum willingly handed over the salmon to Captain Flavel. He took the salmon home and weighed it, finding that the big salmon tipped the scales at ninety-five pounds, an all-time record.

According to Mr. Nolan, members of the Flavel family and neighbors enjoyed eating the record Chinook salmon. Unfortunately, there were no witnesses to the weighing and indeed, no one else heard about the big salmon until years afterwards so there was no way to verify the accuracy of the story.

It would appear that the eighty-four-pound salmon caught for Henry Barbey was probably one of the ten largest salmon ever caught on the river during recorded history.

As seining grounds went, Pillar Rock was not one of the largest but it was a good steady producer of salmon for many years. The crew, working under Chesley Smith, then had about twenty-two men in it with most of them staying at the bunkhouse. Clarence Sigurdson slept on the scow but he would walk up to the bunkhouse occasionally at nights to play cards with other crew members. There wasn't much else to do except to read and sleep, activities most of the seining ground crew indulged in when they weren't working on the seines.

"I remember one time when that island just got loaded with flies," Clarence said. "We would be playing cards and those flies would be everywhere. And, as time passed, there were more and more flies. They would walk over our food and the table and the playing cards. They were everywhere. We used something then called Flystop, or something like that. We sprayed it around with one of those old-time pump sprays and it worked okay on the flies it hit but they just kept coming. Some nights, the floor would be black with dead flies we killed."

The crew finally ran out of fly spray so Chesley Smith told Ralph Edwards, who was running the *Mayday* at that time, to bring back a five-gallon can of Flystop. "We're tired of fooling around with these little one-gallon cans."

When Henry Barbey saw the requisition for a five-gallon can of fly spray, he hit the ceiling. "What do they want with that much fly spray out there anyway?" he asked Edwards.

Edwards answered that the crew was being eaten up by flies and had to have something to kill them with. "Chesley Smith said to get it," he added.

Henry Barbey sighed. "You go back and tell Chesley that he's on an island and any flies on that island are being hatched right there because they can't fly over there from the mainland. Tell Chesley to find the source of the flies, clean that up, and they'll be rid of the flies for good. And you can tell Chesley that he had better do that because I'm not sending him any five-gallon can of Flystop."

After Chesley received the word from Ralph Edwards, he took Clarence Sigurdson with him and the two men tramped around the island looking for the source of the flies.

"We started walking around that island following the beach. It was low tide so we were able to walk right down along the water's edge. We saw something one time that we thought might be it. The cook had been tossing the used bones on the beach so we walked over there to look through the heap but there weren't many flies there so we went on.

"Finally, we came to the manure pile. They kept eight teams of horses in the barn on the scow and each night the men shoveled the manure out and there was a big pile there that ran down to the edge of the water. We got a pitchfork and started digging into that smelly pile and found that it was just a mass of maggots crawling around. It was where the flies were coming from, all right."

Chesley Smith ordered a big sled to be built and then hitched one of the teams to that sled and began hauling that old manure out into the water where the sled would be dumped and brought back for another load. It all washed down the river and any maggots in it were soon eaten by fish so it was an ecologically-sound procedure, even for that time. The pile soon disappeared and after that, all of the manure from the barn was always dumped into the river immediately.

"Funny thing," Clarence said, "but nobody out there even thought about finding out where the flies were coming from but Henry Barbey did the first time he heard about it. He was a pretty sharp man to work for."

Daily life at the Pillar Rock seining grounds was scheduled around the tides. When they were right for seining, every man on the island would be busy at his own particular job and would keep going until the tide changed at which time all of the gear was taken out of the water and put away until the next tide. The horses would be taken to the barn for rest and food, and the men on the island would relax until it was time to go out again. Each day, the tide changed at a different hour, roughly an hour later than the day before, so the daily routine varied from day to day.

It was an odd life for a young man to live and yet every seining ground had a waiting list of men wanting to work there. They received good money for the time and were provided with all of life's necessities so most of them were able to save almost all of that season's wages. It was a perfect setup for a college boy and many of them took advantage of that fact. They worked year after year on the seining grounds while they went back to college in the fall, living on the put-aside wages of the summer's work.

Graham Barbey said later, "I can recall in later times when many men came up to my father at social gatherings and introduced themselves and told my father that if it hadn't been for him giving them a job on the seining grounds, they never would have been able to make it through college during those Depression days."

Graham himself worked on the seining grounds on Welch's Sands during his Stanford college days. "They were great days in the fishing industry along the lower Columbia River then. We got $2.50 a day and I can remember one time the workers had a kind of strike and made up a chant which they used. 'Three dollars a day or Barbey in the bay!' I think that was on Sand Island.

"I can also recall the meals were great. Ham and eggs and hot cakes. There was so much food you couldn't possibly eat it all for breakfast. Any time the seine crew pulled in over one hundred tons of salmon in one day, they were paid for two days. This didn't happen too often but there was an awful lot of fish caught back in those days."

Pillar Rock Sands was one of the best seining grounds on the lower Columbia River and was operated by the Barbey Packing Co. from 1930 until seining was legislated out of existence in Oregon. The last year that Barbey seined there was in 1950. After that, all fish canned at the various canneries on both sides of river was caught either by gillnetters or by off-shore trollers.

The elimination of the seining grounds removed forever one of the most interesting methods of fishing ever devised and brought an end to a constant source of salmon for the canneries. It also eliminated an entire class of skilled fishermen who fished in a manner almost unknown in other parts of the world.

It was a rare seining season when the local police or sheriff's office didn't get a call from a tourist telling them that there had been some kind of disaster out in the river. "I can see men and horses struggling out there in the water," they would cry. "And there are some boats out there trying to help them." Each time, the patient police would tell the tourist that the men in the river were in no danger at all — they were just fishing.

Looking back, it was an incredible method of fishing.

Chapter 17

BARBEY, RABBIT ISLAND, AND THE BROWNS

Rabbit Island in the Columbia River just down from Celilo Falls was an island only during the spring freshets when the flood waters of the river roared down the gorge, built to new heights by the outpourings of a hundred smaller rivers and creeks emptying the melted snow packs of the high country. The rest of the year, Rabbit Island was connected to the state of Washington by a rocky road winding its way from the shoreline to the island over a surface of rocks of all sizes.

F.C. "Cap" Brown, his wife, and two children lived on Rabbit Island in a house built of rocks, trimmed with wood, and chinked with concrete. "Cap" had been the skipper of one of the Oregon Fish Commission boats, but had left that job to go into gillnetting on the upper river and had been staying on Rabbit Island. Barbey had known "Cap" for many years so it was natural that when Barbey looked to the mid-river area near The Dalles as a source of additional fresh salmon and bought Rabbit Island, he hired "Cap" to continue living on the island and at the same time, take charge of his fishing operations there for him.

Henry Barbey said later, "I bought salmon from fish wheels at Celilo, Oregon for a number of years but decided in about 1922 to find a good location and build my own fish wheel. I knew of a likely location on the Washington side of the Columbia River near Avery, Washington, on Rabbit Island. I knew I could have a buying station at this location and also a seining ground operation but wished to purchase enough land so I could take the salmon I purchased and the salmon I caught to the railroad station at Avery, so I could ship to my cannery at Flavel.

Some of the stone fishermen's cabins on Rabbit Island. (Photo courtesy D. Sutter, Arcadia, Calif.)

"Mr. F.C. "Cap" Brown was then gillnetting near Avery and was staying on Rabbit Island so I saw him and told him that I was considering building a fish wheel on the island and wanted to know if he could look after the construction of this wheel."

"He wanted to know if he could have a half interest in this wheel. He had no money to invest but would pay one half the cost of the fish wheel from his share of the catch of salmon, and would also look after its construction and operation."

In 1924, Henry Barbey bought twenty-seven acres of land on the island from Sarah Starkley. This was the land on which Brown had built his house, and was also the land on which the fishwheel was eventually built, as well as all other later improvements because all of this first twenty-seven acres was above extreme high water. In 1926, Barbey bought an additional sixty-two acres from Quincy Newkirk, and in 1927, purchased the remaining thirty-two acres from C.L. Spanggard. This gave him title to the entire island. Barbey told "Cap" Brown that he would have to buy a half interest in this land and in any improvements made on the island but he could pay for it out of his part of the profits of the operations. In 1940, Brown completed his contract and received a deed for half of the land and improvements on Rabbit Island.

Henry Barbey built a mess house and bunk houses which were used to house and feed his seining-ground crews who came to the island to fish. At times, the bunk houses were also used by gillnet fishermen who used the island as their headquarters while the fishing season was on. Brown was to keep the rent from these for acting as caretaker of all the property on the island. Brown also received a commission for buying and handling the gillnet-caught fish.

Since Henry Barbey was to build the mess house and bunk houses at his own expense, he stipulated that "Cap" Brown was to build five or six one-room rock houses for the gillnetters and for tourists to use after the fishing season was over.

Brown had an unlimited supply of rocks to use for the construction of these houses so he set to work on what was to become one of the most unusual villages in the Pacific Northwest.

It was said that one of the members of the fishing crew was a Swedish architect who became interested in Brown's problem and assisted him in devising a method of construction which could be used. He showed Brown how to pyramid the stone so that the weight of the rocks themselves bound them together without the use of mortar.

While he was building his six smaller houses, "Cap" also worked on his own home, eventually turning it into a six room house, complete with fireplace and a penthouse-type bedroom perched on top of the main house. When it was completed, it was named "Bunny's Castle" after his pet name for his wife.

Barbey, like all of the other independent salmon packers on the river, was always looking for new sources of fresh salmon. The elimination of the purse seiners in the early 1920s cut deep into Barbey's yearly salmon supply so it was essential that he find more salmon to can if he was to stay in business.

"Bunny's Castle" on Rabbit Island, built by "Cap" Brown as the family residence. (Photo courtesy D. Sutter, Arcadia, Calif.)

Most of the gillnetters on the lower Columbia river were tied to the old-line packers by contracts while most of the seining grounds were already being leased by the same packers. It was difficult for a new packing firm to acquire new permanent sources of salmon under these conditions.

The mid-river fishing area between The Dalles and Celilo Falls was also tied up in the early 1920s. The Seufert family had moved into the area and had built their first fish wheel on the river there in 1885 and for the next twenty years built and bought many other wheels. Seuferts also bought salmon from the Indians who fished the falls at Celilo with dipnets using methods handed down for hundreds of years. On the face of it, the area near The Dalles looked no more promising for a new salmon packer than did the lower river near Astoria.

The salmon fisheries at this point on the Columbia River was different from what it was two hundred miles to the west. Here, the Columbia River roared its way around and over rocks. The river was divided into a hundred different

"Cap" Brown's office on Rabbit Island. (Photo courtesy D. Sutter, Arcadia, Calif.)

courses of water, some moving swiftly through deep rock gullies while other water poured over falls and rapids. The salmon still had to move through this maze but in different ways than they did in the deep wide waters near the mouth.

The spawning ground-bound salmon came to this point in their journey and found that they had to move through narrow channels in the rock where huge fish wheels turned with the current, scooping them up as they passed under the moving wheel. They had to leap foaming cataracts where the Indians with dip nets waited to pull them out of the water as they moved past. There were some quiet areas between the rapids but even here, gillnetters and seiners operated and caught their share of the migrating fish.

Primarily, the fisheries at The Dalles was an autumn operation. It opened usually about September 10th and lasted approximately six weeks. This was the time when the big Chinooks came through on their way to their spawning grounds and at this time they were still prime fish with a good color and a high fat content. These were called channel fish because they had escaped the gillnetters in the lower river by swimming in the channel and were heading for their spawning grounds hundreds of miles up the Snake River. They were excellent quality in the month of September whereas the salmon caught in the lower river were poor quality as they were heading for spawning grounds near the mouth of the river and nature knew they didn't have the strength for a long swim. The Chinooks would lose weight and fat and, by the time they reached their goal, the salmon would be gaunt and weakened by their journey up the Columbia River.

One of the reasons that Henry Barbey bought Rabbit Island was because there was a chute there bordering the south side of the island where the water ran swift and deep between the Oregon shore and Rabbit Island. He had seen an Indian standing on the rock edge of this chute with a dip net and had seen him scooping up salmon as they passed between the steep sides of the chute.

"Build the fishwheel there, "Cap"," he said, "and we should catch enough salmon in it in one year to pay for the wheel. After that it is all pure profit."

The two men did build a wheel which cost Henry Barbey about $10,000 to install. The first year, the wheel caught enough salmon to more than pay the cost of installing it. It operated until the fish wheels were declared illegal by Oregon in 1927 by an initiative placed on the ballot by the gillnetters, the Oregon State Grange, Oregon Federation of Labor, and Oregon Fish Commission. All of the Astoria salmon packers opposed it except for Union Fish. After the initiative was passed, the Rabbit Island fish wheel was tied down and eventually was swept away during one of the Columbia River's periodic floods. This same legislation practically put the Seuferts out of the salmon canning business.

The State of Washington also passed legislation in 1934, eliminating all fixed gear, fishwheels, traps, seines, and set nets which virtually ended Washington fishing on the Columbia River although this legislation was primarily aimed at Puget Sound fisheries. From this time on, Rabbit Island was used by the middle-river gillnetters for putting their boats into the water so they could gillnet in that area.

Fish wheels had been tried on the lower reaches of the Columbia River at times but they were not successful there because of the lack of the swift, narrow water passages needed to operate the machines so the Oregon fishwheel legislation was primarily aimed at the upriver fisheries.

Rabbit Island also had a flat, rocky beach which extended smoothly down into the river making it an ideal site for a seining ground. Barbey found a farmer who had horses that could be used on a seining ground. He lived near Maryhill and would bring his horse teams to Rabbit Island each year to be used on the seining ground and then, when the salmon season was over, would take his horses back to his Washington ranch until the next season rolled around.

There were gillnetters operating in that area and Barbey arranged to buy as much salmon from them as he could, paying highest prices and cash as was his usual custom. He soon built up a reliable source of fresh salmon in that area which he used in his Flavel cannery to fill in during the fall of each year. Barbey leased a protected harbor at the head of Eightmile Rapids and the gillnetters of the area worked out of this harbor, selling their catch to Barbey and at times to others. There was no way that Barbey or any other packer could force the independent gillnetters to sell to him exclusively, but when they used Rabbit Island to put their boats into the water and to store their trailers, Mrs. Brown, who had taken over after "Cap" Brown's death, insisted that these fishermen deliver their fish to her. Barbey paid her a commission per pound for buying for him and this money enabled her to support herself.

"Cap" Brown operated the fishwheel while it was legal but there were other duties to be performed so Barbey usually sent one of his men up to Rabbit Island each year to assist Brown and to do other things to get the Barbey Packing Co. more fresh salmon.

In the early 1930s, Barbey summoned one of his crew, a young man named Clarence Sigurdson of Warrenton, and asked him if he would like to go up to Rabbit Island for the fall salmon run to assist "Cap" Brown with the fishing operations there. Clarence had been working for Barbey at his Pillar Rock seining grounds and jumped at the chance to try something new.

"The first year," Clarence said later, "I drove up to Rabbit Island or Brown's Island as we sometimes called it. I took a ferry across the river from The Dalles, Oregon, to Dallesport, Washington. I had a car and I drove up to Wishram, Washington. A good part of that road went straight up the sides of the Washington hills.

"When I got to the island, Brown assigned me a cabin but most of the other help lived in a bunkhouse except for the Browns who lived in their rock house. I drove out there over that rocky road because it was in the fall and the river was low. I don't know how Brown got back and forth during the spring when the freshet was on. Seems like he was pretty well marooned there in the spring.

"My duties were simple enough. I had one man under me who butchered the fish and another guy who drove the truck back and forth with the fish. The butcher did his job right out in the open air in those days but I guess you couldn't do that now."

The railroad had a siding there and a little building and it was called the Avery flag stop. Clarence would put up a flag when he wanted the train to stop and pick up a rail carload of fish for delivery to Astoria, Oregon.

Clarence would go to Wishram, Washington, and order a freight car spotted at Avery. "I didn't give them any money," he said, "so I guess Barbey had made arrangements with them. The railroad would bring over a refrigerated car from the Northwest Ice and Cold Storage Co. in Portland loaded with about seven tons of ice. When the car was filled with salmon, the ice would be all through it.

"The car would be quite long and every ten feet or so, we would nail up a 2 x 4 wall. We piled in the salmon like cordwood clear up to the top and then started another pile with another 2 x 4 barrier. Eventually, there would be about 20 tons of salmon in each car. When the car was filled, the railroad would stop a train and pick up the car up and haul it down to the Astoria cannery where the salmon would be canned.

"These salmon were caught in the seining grounds in the early days and later by gillnetters. Brown didn't deal with the Indians then. I guess Seufert had them all tied up or something."

Clarence Sigurdson, who lives in Seaside now, chuckles as he recalls those long-ago days on Rabbit Island. "The second year I went up there. I thought I would trade my car in so I took the train, got off at Avery, and was met by "Cap" Brown's daughter Eleanor. She was a mighty pretty girl then, pretty enough to be in the movies.

"Actually, I found out later that Eleanor Brown was a movie star during the early days and caught on because of her looks. She played one of the leads in that film *East Lynne* with Ann Harding, a top Hollywood star then.

"The Browns were nice people and they used to invite me to come up to their house and have dinner with them. It was then that they told me about Eleanor's Hollywood adventures. They went down to Hollywood one time, "Cap" and his wife, to see Eleanor at work. It seems that when they were leaving, Eleanor said, 'Well, so long, "Cap"!' as they were leaving and the director of the picture she was working on heard that and asked if her father really was a captain."

"Sure, he's a captain," Eleanor said.

"Well, we need a captain in this next scene we're shooting," the director said. They fitted "Cap" out in a natty blue captain's uniform and put him up on a fake gangplank and had him come down that plank and escort Ann Harding, the star of the picture, up to the ship. "It was the easiest $350 I ever made," "Cap" chuckled later.

Unfortunately for Eleanor, the talkies came along about then and they soon found out that her voice was not at all suitable for the new type of moving pictures so that was the end of her career as a movie star. She left Hollywood and returned to Rabbit Island in the early 1930s.

Clarence Sigurdson still recalls those quiet evenings at the Browns' dinner table. " "Cap" used to tell me about things that happened on Rabbit Island in the old days and one time he took me out to the north end of the island and showed me an iron bar which had been drilled into the rock there.

There was a chute there running between the island and the Washington shore where the water ran right up on edge and you could see a log coming down and it would go into a whirlpool, disappear, and come up again about 300 feet down the river.

"He was telling me about a time when CRPA — they had a seining ground just above him — decided to take a boat through that chute. It was loaded down with supplies from Astoria for the seining grounds and if they could boat it up there, they wouldn't have to bother with trucking it at all.

" "Cap" heard about it and came out and drilled a hole in the rock and pushed that big iron bar in there tight. He tied a rope around it and put a life preserver on the end and waited for the CRPA boat to make the run up the chute. It came up all right but halfway through the chute it hit a whirlpool which took the boat and slammed it up against the rocks, busted it up, and wrecked and sunk it. "Cap" said he saw some of the men trying to swim in that maelstrom so he tossed in the life preserver and pulled them out, one by one. I guess that was the only time anyone tried to run a boat up that particular chute."

Sigurdson was there running the shipping operations for two years and then went on to other things. He returned later — 1935, he thinks it was — and dropped in to see his friends, the Browns. He spent one night with them and while there "Cap" told him what had been happening on Rabbit Island since he left.

Bonneville Dam down river from The Dalles was then being planned and a group of engineers visited Rabbit Island to pick up samples of rock found there. They had been going up and down the river, looking for a gravel deposit big enough and good enough to use to build the dam. They came to Rabbit Island to look at the seining ground gravel there.

There was one young fellow who worked with the engineers and while they stayed on the island, he became quite friendly with the Brown's son. Mrs. Brown saw this and she went to the engineers and said, "If you fellows want to, I've got this cookhouse and the bunkhouse here which we only use during the seining ground season. You can stay here and I'll cook for you and charge you a reasonable amount for board and room." They took her up on that and stayed for more than a week.

The young fellow came to "Cap" and told him that the company building Bonneville Dam was thinking seriously of making some kind of a deal with Mr. Barbey to get rocks off Rabbit Island for Bonneville. He said, "They will pay plenty so you should make up your mind as to how much you want for the rocks — just a set price."

Mrs. Brown said later that she and "Cap" stayed up nights, trying to make up their minds about how much to tell Barbey to ask for the rock. If they went too high, he might lose the deal and if they went too low, he would lose money, so they thought and thought and finally decided that maybe ten or fifteen thousand would be about right. They went to the young fellow and told him what they were going to recommend and he told them they were thinking too low. "Fifteen thousand is nothing", he said. "They will have to pay to haul the rock from elsewhere so they are willing to pay plenty for your rock."

The Browns telephoned Barbey about the deal since he owned the island. Almost immediately, he called back saying that they should hold out for $100,000 and accept nothing lower. That was a lot of money back in the Depression days of the 1930s but the Browns took a chance and told the engineers that they could have their rock for that figure and no other. To their surprise, their offer was accepted and Henry Barbey was considerably ahead on his Rabbit Island investment.

Later, Mrs. Brown said, "And that wasn't all either. When they started scooping out that gravel, I had all of that crew staying here in our bunkhouse and I was feeding them and charging them for their board and room. I made pretty good money for myself that way."

Clarence Sigurdson asked "Cap" Brown if taking all that rock from the Rabbit Island seining ground hadn't hurt the grounds. "Not a bit," "Cap" grinned. "They took all the rock and left a big hole but the next freshet that came along leveled all of it nice and smooth again and brought in more gravel and the seining there was just as good as it had ever been."

After seining was outlawed, the Barbey fisheries operation on Rabbit Island continued although now he had to buy the salmon from the gillnetters who were still fishing there.

When The Dalles Dam was being built, the government bought out the Seufert cannery and all of the Indian fish cables which Seufert had constructed to carry the Indians from the shore to the islands in the middle of the river. These were steel cables and the Indians rode in fish boxes high over the raging waters of the Columbia River below to their fishing stations.

All of these cables were put up for bid and Barbey's bid was the highest so they had the use of many of the Seuferts cables for about three years. Graham Barbey recalled that they were getting about seventy-thousand pounds of salmon from cables daily. "Incredible!" he said later.

Construction of The Dalles Dam brought an end to the saga of Rabbit Island because the lake behind the dam eventually covered most of the island. One more amusing story did come out of this final act. It seems that a crew of army engineers were inspecting the island to determine its worth since they would have to pay the owners if it was to be covered with water. Mrs. Brown was in her rock house and overheard the men talking about how the island was owned by a little old lady — "Cap" Brown had died by this time — and it should not be difficult to get the island for a steal.

When Henry Barbey retired, he gave half of Rabbit Island to his son Graham and the other half to "Cap" Brown in recognition of his many years of service to the Barbey Packing Company. Actually, Barbey did not think the island was of much value because by this time seining grounds had been outlawed in both Oregon and Washington. However, Mrs. Brown still had her rock houses available for the sport fishermen and had her home there as well so she welcomed the gift.

The Corps of Engineers made a token offer of $10,000 for the island but Mrs. Brown called Graham Barbey in Astoria to explain the situation and said, "You've got to come up here and stop them from stealing our property."

Graham assured her that they would do no such thing. He and Mrs. Brown entered a joint suit against the Engineers asking for $200,000 damages in Federal Court at Yakima, Washington. Their attorneys put Mrs. Brown on the witness stand, dressed meekly in black. She wore a black veil and cried while telling the court that the government was taking her little houses and island from her, offering her only $10,000 for her home. The court awarded Mrs. Brown and Graham Barbey ten times the Army Engineers' first offer, which they divided evenly.

"Anyway," Graham Barbey said later, "we still own Rabbit Island, what there is left of it. I think there are still about fourteen acres of it above low water that we pay property taxes on."

While the mid-river fisheries at The Dalles and Celilo were never of supreme importance to the well-being of the Barbey Packing Co.'s operations, they did provide extra salmon during the times when the downriver fisheries were more or less dormant. Rabbit Island with its fish wheel, seining ground and gillnetters provided Henry Barbey and later his son Graham with occasional financial opportunities and was a doorway into the mid-river fishing area.

In the career of an independent salmon packer, all sources of salmon no matter how obscure were important to his over-all operation if he was to remain in business competitively.

Chapter 18

BARBEY AND THE ALBACORE TUNA

Astorians have always centered their thinking around salmon. They think salmon, work salmon, and live salmon all year long. When the salmon are running, the town settles down into a routine built around the fishing, the weather, the tides, and the canneries. During the winter season, they talk about the past year's catch and look forward to the coming one.

Because of this concentration on one basic natural resource, Astorians may be excused for not instantly recognizing a new marine resource which suddenly appeared in the town in 1936. It was a new fish, strange in appearance, and caught using a new method of fishing, but who cared? Salmon was king and there was no room for a possible successor.

So it was no wonder that hardly anyone in Astoria paid the slightest bit of attention to the first seven tons of albacore tuna which were delivered to the docks of Arthur Anderson's Columbia River Salmon Co. in 1936. The load of strange fish was a freak catch and was treated like one. None of the canneries in Astoria knew what to do with the fish so the odd catch was shipped to California for processing and that was that. The poor skipper of the troller who brought the fish in was regarded with some pity for wasting his time with such a load of fish but it really was not his fault. He and his crew had been trolling off shore for salmon, farther out than salmon normally moved. The fishing had been poor in close to the shore and they had moved farther out from shore in hopes of finding some salmon there. The captain steered westward and they suddenly found themselves in the middle of a big school of albacore tuna.

The crew, for want of something better to do, started casting lines with lures on them into the water and were astounded to find that the albacore would bite on almost anything. As soon as they hauled one tuna in, another would be waiting to bite. The crew fished for several hours, enjoying themselves immensely, and suddenly found themselves awash in seven tons of albacore tuna. Luckily, one of the men aboard recognized the odd fish for what it was and told the skipper that they could be sold if they could get them in to shore as soon as possible. The skipper turned his boat eastward and within a few hours docked it at Arthur Anderson's cannery dock at Astoria. The rest is history.

The following year, the ocean salmon trollers had been having a poor season with small catches prevailing throughout the fishing fleet. The off-shore trollers had tried almost everything they could think of including the use of new types of lures and different methods of fishing for the ocean salmon but the salt water salmon still did not bite in any great quantity. Eventually, a few trollers headed farther west to try out there for the elusive salmon but found instead more schools of albacore tuna. A few boats paused there to fish for the strange fish and soon the fishing docks at Astoria were receiving big loads of albacore tuna.

The tuna canning industry up to this time had been centered in California where various kinds of tuna had been canned since 1912. Of all the tunas caught, the white-meated albacore was the most prized, but other kinds such as yellowfin, bluefin, skipjack and bonito were also canned although their darker flesh made them less desirable to the consumer than the white albacore.

The albacore tends to swim with the Japanese current which flows close to the coast of California. It was thought that in 1936, the current came in closer to the coast of Oregon than in earlier years and had brought the albacore in with it.

Because of the poor salmon trolling conditions of 1937, more attention was paid to the new fish. Samples were sent to the Oregon State Seafood Laboratory at Astoria and were promptly identified as albacore tuna, the finest white-meated tuna available.

After reading the laboratory's report, a few of the more progressive salmon packers began to make preparations for an experimental pack. The albacore tuna were coming into the salmon docks in quantity now and it was obvious to the fish-wise packers of Astoria that there was more money to be made in canning albacore tuna in their own canneries than in sending the fish to California for processing.

Astoria, however, was a salmon town and no one there in the fish processing business knew much about the albacore tuna. There was much to learn before the packers could go into this untried venture. The fishermen had learned that the tuna had to be bled immediately after being caught to preserve the whiteness of the tuna flesh, and, since the tuna were caught farther out on the ocean than the salmon had been, new methods of preserving the fish temporarily until they could be delivered to the canneries had to be developed.

The Astoria salmon packers soon found that there were many differences between canning tuna and salmon. Salmon, for example, is put into the cans raw and then cooked whereas the albacore has to be precooked before processing. The packing of the cans is done differently, as is the cleaning and the grading. No one locally had any knowledge of these things so the packers had to go to California for expert help.

Henry Barbey went to Terminal Island in California to interview people familiar with the tuna packing industry. He hired Mr. and Mrs. Ben Nicholson of Long Beach, California to come north to Astoria to manage his proposed new albacore tuna packing facility. The Nicholsons moved to Astoria and with Henry Barbey they spent the next few months planning future tuna operations.

Henry Barbey had always been a cautious man who would gamble, but only when he had examined every facet of a proposition and had found that the odds were in his favor. In the case of the albacore tuna, he felt that a trial pack using as much of his present facility as possible was best. Therefore, the first year, the Barbey Packing Co. put up a small experimental pack.

The results of that initial albacore tuna pack was so satisfactory that Henry Barbey decided that he could safely

The Barbey Packing Co. cannery at Astoria. The albacore tuna section is on the left while the salmon section is at right center. The two-story part at center is the office area. (Photo courtesy Columbia River Maritime Museum)

enter the tuna packing field. In August of 1939, he announced plans to build a new tuna cannery adjoining the Barbey Packing Co. salmon cannery near Pier 1, on the Port of Astoria.

He built the new 250 by 50 foot wooden building on pilings above the river on the south side of the salmon cannery and connected the two buildings so access from one to another was easy. Certain parts of the salmon cannery such as the business office, cold rooms and the docks, would serve both the tuna and the salmon operations and some of the work crews could be moved from one operation to the other rapidly and without confusion.

It is interesting to note that CRPA was at that time completing a new cold storage plant, and work on their tuna cannery addition was also progressing rapidly. At the Union Fishermen's Cooperative Packing Company, a crew was rushing to completion a tuna packing unit with two lines. The Columbia River Salmon Company as well as the Point Adams Packing Company were also proclaiming increased production and New England Fish Co. announced that tuna would be processed that year. Almost every salmon packer in town was moving towards a double operation of salmon and albacore tuna. It was the beginning of a new era for Astoria.

It was about this time that Henry Barbey was closing down the Allen and Hendrickson stringbean cannery at Rainier so he had the boilers and retorts from that facility taken to Astoria to use in the new tuna cannery. He also sent tables and other equipment down to Astoria for use in his new two-line tuna cannery which was designed for the processing of fifty tons of albacore tuna a day.

After the tuna cannery was erected and equipped, ready for the coming season's operation, Mr. and Mrs. Ben Nicholson began training Barbey's workers to handle the new fish. Experienced cannery workers trained in salmon canning had to learn the new processes before the cannery could operate.

"The routine went like this," Graham Barbey said. "The stomach of the tuna was cleaned out first and then the tuna was put into wire baskets and placed in the pre-cookers or retorts — we had four of them — and the tuna cooked in there for 4½ hours at approximately 350 degrees. The length of cook and temperature depended on the size of the tuna."

Women did most of the actual handling of the tuna after it had been pre-cooked and cooled. A woman, usually older and skilled in all phases of preparing albacore tuna for packing and experienced in cannery work, was in charge of the women and was called the floor lady. She worked directly under the Barbeys and was responsible for keeping the flow of tuna moving along from one phase to another. The skinners were given the whole cooked tuna and their job was to clean the black skin off and remove the heads and tails. The carcass then went to the cleaners who took out the backbone, separated the body into four parts and scraped these long, white, solid pieces of albacore tuna immaculately clean. The sections of the fish were then placed on cutting boards and run through a guillotine knife which cut the cleaned tuna into the correct size for the cans. These pieces then went to the packers who filled the cans using the large pieces for the solid pack. This was called hand pack.

At first, solid pack was the top grade, followed by broken pieces called flakes, and finally dark and white flakes. There were three grades during the early days but later this was changed to solid pack, chunk style, and dark and white tuna. The flakes disappeared from the labels.

An expert hand packer could fill a can with one large piece and a few small bits tucked in at the last minute to bring the can up to the proper weight. Each can was placed on small individual scales and the filled can had to be heavier than a counter weight placed on the other side of the scale. When the packer was satisfied that the can was filled properly, she placed it on a moving belt which transported it to an endless chain which took the can through a salter which deposited a small bit of salt in each can automatically, through an oiler which dropped in a small amount of soybean or cottonseed oil, and through the lidder which placed a lid on each open can. An identification code was stamped on each lid and then the can moved through a sealer and was moved into the retort for cooking. Later, it was transported to another part of the cannery for labeling and boxing.

After the cooked tuna had been removed from the wire baskets, the baskets and racks were dipped into a hot lye bath to clean them, and then were hosed off and were ready to be used again.

Many of the processes of preparing and canning the albacore tuna had to be learned and refined by the local packers to fit the local conditions. For example, Graham Barbey said this about adding oil to the packed tuna:

"When we first started canning albacore tuna, we copied what they were doing in California at that time. They were adding cottonseed oil to the cans and what we learned is that when you take tuna and put it into a can with water in it, it has no flavor whatsoever. If it was immersed in cottonseed oil for six months on the shelf, you had a flavor that you figured was canned tuna. During World War II, all of a sudden there wasn't any cottonseed oil available so the canners switched to soybean oil and the flavor was so similar that the housewife didn't notice the difference."

*Henry and Ethel Barbey on a vacation cruise to Hawaii in 1938 on
the* SS Lurline.

In the beginning, all tuna in Astoria was hand-packed in
seven or 6½ ounce cans but later a local man named Eben
Carruthers invented a tuna filling machine which revolution-
ized the industry and hand packing tuna became almost a
thing of the past.

Everyone who ever worked at Barbeys agreed that they
put out a quality pack. Jim Ferguson said, "Barbeys, you
know, always was a hand-packed operation and based upon
a high quality product. Our tuna was beautifully packed —
very fancy — and the market at that time was limited because
there was a lot of imports coming in but even so, the Barbeys
never cut down on the quality of the albacore tuna — or
the salmon either, for that matter."

Esther Rinne, the floor lady, agreed. "He was the nicest
man — Henry that is — but his son Graham was always
so finicky about quality when we were working. I remember
once we had two real nice looking tuna but I said to Mr.
Barbey, 'They smell!' and he said that they smelled okay to

him. Later, Graham came along and he smelled them too and said, 'Throw them in the river!' so I did and then Henry came back and he said, 'Where's my fish?' I told him that they went into the river — they didn't like it here. He just laughed. He knew what had happened."

"He didn't care if the girls worked fast. He just wanted them to do good work. That's why I liked him. He would walk around the place in those beautiful grey suits he always wore, carrying his glasses in his hand, and when he wanted to see something up close, he would put the glasses on for a moment, peer at whatever he was trying to see, and then go on, glasses in hand again."

Esther Rinne smiled as she remembered those long ago days at the Barbey Packing Co. "He was particular with salmon too. The slices of salmon had to be put into the cans in a certain way so they would fit perfectly. The skin would always be on the outside, next to the can sides — never in the middle. You had to know how to put the salmon into the cans."

"But I never did hear him bawl anyone out or even raise his voice. He just looked but he never seemed to miss anything that went on, even though he never said anything about it. He would compliment but never complain. He was a wonderful man."

Mrs. Rinne went on. "I liked Graham too because he was always so kind. I remember once I was sitting out on the dock eating my lunch. It was a real nice day and I was just sitting there. I put my sandwich down on my lap for a moment and, believe it or not, a seagull swooped down and took my sandwich away from me. Graham saw that and laughed and laughed. I said, 'Don't laugh. I lost my sandwich'. So he said, 'Don't worry. I'll go and get you another one'. He took his car and drove all the way downtown just to get me a new sandwich. He was real nice to me and to all of the girls."

In many ways, packing albacore tuna was much easier than salmon. For example, the packers rarely had to supply the unprocessed fish as they did in salmon where they had to maintain and operate seining ground, fish wheels, traps, and fleets of gillnetters. The tuna was brought to the canneries by the tuna boats many of them from California. These large refrigerated tuna boats or clippers as many of them were called, could range far out to sea and were capable of staying out there for days and even weeks at a time. Of course, to accommodate these large boats, icing facilities and additional unloading docks with hoists had to be built at each cannery, but it was a good trade-off for the packers.

"When the albacore tuna first started in our area," Graham Barbey said, "the boats went out only for the day and caught the tuna within fifty miles offshore. They would bring the fish in iced, just like they did with troll salmon."

"Later, they found that the albacore were farther out so they had to get shelf freezers in the boats. The tuna would be laid on the shelf and then were frozen. Operating that way, the boats could stay out maybe four or five days. Later, they found that they could dump the tuna in water and salt — brine, it was called, and they would freeze solid. After that, the local boats could stay out even longer and range farther offshore where the big schools of albacore were to be found.

"These tuna boats at that time cost about $175,000 but soon the fishermen decided that it was not economical to go out there in such a small boat when a bigger one could stay out longer and bring in more tuna so they started building two-million-dollar boats and then even five-million-dollar ones. These boats would go out maybe twice a year and if they got a big load, they made a real bundle. If not, they could always hope the next time out would be better."

Eventually, the Barbey Packing Co. started buying frozen albacore tuna from Japan to supplement the local fishermen's catches. This Japanese tuna was shipped to Astoria in merchant ships which had refrigerated holds. Some years, there was so much locally-caught albacore tuna that the canneries were as much as seven days behind in unloading the tuna boats waiting to deliver to the canneries in Astoria.

"It was a constantly changing scene," Graham Barbey said. "First, we got all the local tuna we could get in fresh and after that we got in the tuna frozen. About that time, the boats from California came up here because the albacore that had been down in that area moved up here.

Henry and Ethel Barbey at a formal dinner party in Beverly Hills in 1940.

In California, they sold to Van Camp but when they got here, they sold some of the catch to us. Actually, some of these boats should have taken it all back down to California because whoever was financing them was there and wanted that fish, but the boats were here so they delivered to us and to CRPA but would take their last load back to California."

"Sometimes we had so much tuna coming in from these boats that we were eight days behind in unloading them. We would take their order and they would wait in either the upper or lower mooring basin until we sent word that we were ready for them. We would take them in the order they signed in."

Below is the reported annual albacore tuna packs of the Barbey Packing Co. It is interesting to note the drop in production during the war years.

1939 - 10,500 cases	1947 - 4,709 cases
1940 - 20,160 cases	1948 - 6,860 cases
1941 - 19,000 cases	1949 - 9,835 cases
1942 - 18,000 cases	1950 - 10,100 cases
1943 - 9,075 cases	1951 - 8,436 cases
1944 - 4,219 cases	1952 - 6,883 cases
1945 - 2,680 cases	1953 - 6,562 cases
1946 - 756 cases	1954 - 8,292 cases

The Barbey Packing Corp. finally gave up packing albacore tuna. Graham Barbey explains why;

"When we first started packing albacore tuna, we canned and sold some of it under buyer's label and some under the Barbey label but it was difficult for us to can enough tuna to compete with the big boys — we're talking here about Star Kist and Chicken of the Sea. We therefore decided that we would ship frozen tuna down to them and they paid us $50 a ton for shipping it to them. Some days, we would buy $100,000 worth of tuna for them and ship it down to them by truck. It usually arrived there with two days. It cost us about $5 a ton to handle it and we didn't have the expense of canning or financing it so it was quite profitable.

"For some reason, the albacore tuna disappeared for awhile from this area and we just could not get enough to run the cannery profitably so we had to import it from Japan and that made it pretty expensive. We therefore decided that we could make more money by buying what we could and shipping it to California to Van Camp and Star Kist."

The albacore tuna packing years in Astoria lasted for more than twenty years and provided a much-needed boost to the salmon packers at a time when the salmon catch was beginning to decline rapidly because of the dams and pollution. Albacore tuna gave them a new product to can and undoubtedly was responsible for keeping some of them operating years after they would have closed had the tuna not arrived off the Oregon coast.

But, like the salmon, the albacore tuna also began to disappear. The annual pack became smaller and less profitable until finally, it, like the salmon, disappeared completely from Astoria's economic scene, taking with it a part of Astoria's color and interest as well as one of its sources of employment. This was one of the reasons for the sad decline of the ancient town at the mouth of the Columbia River, leaving only memories of a once-better day.

Chapter 19

THE WAR YEARS AT THE
BARBEY PACKING CO.

The beginning of World War II brought many changes to Astoria and to the people who lived there and in the surrounding Lower Columbia area. The Japanese attack on Pearl Harbor on Dec. 7, 1941 brought an instant wave of fear to local residents on both sides of the river. The lights went out and the town virtually closed down tight as the people waited to see what the enemy would do next. There was nothing between the mouth of the Columbia River and Hawaii except bare ocean and fully half the town expected the next attack to hit Astoria.

As the days passed without incident, the people began to relax and go about their business as usual but the sudden regulations put into effect locally by the Coast Guard and the US Navy did remind them that there was a war on and that the mouth of the Columbia River was at that time a point of possible enemy action. Blackouts were enforced and cars running at night had to have headlight dimmers installed which made night driving extremely hazardous.

Along the waterfront, usually well-lighted at all hours, the sudden darkness curtailed much of the activities of the marine-related businesses and industries. Because it was December, however, cannery activity was at a minimum but war regulations slowed even that to a virtual halt.

The Japanese population of Astoria had never been too large. A few came into the county before 1900 but by 1920 there were still only 437 Japanese residents according to the census. On December 8, the *Astorian Budget* said that there were thirty-seven Japanese living in the county on that date:

one in Seaside, eleven in Hammond and the rest in Astoria. These Orientals were unobtrusive and kept together and at no time was their presence of great importance to the economy of the area. The men generally worked in mills or in the canneries but always in small numbers.

Relations between the local Japanese and other residents had always been friendly. Astoria has always been a cosmopolitan town with a constantly fluctuating type of population and its residents had become accustomed to working with and living near other races without any extreme problems of prejudice. In May of 1942 when the last local Japanese left on chartered busses for the government relocation camps, there were many sincere expressions of regret from other Astorians although there were also undoubtedly sighs of relief from those who had feared possible sabotage and spying activity because of the unknown war feelings of all Japanese.

Certainly, the departure of the local Japanese caused no hardship to the cannery owners because there never were enough of them working in any one cannery to become a significant part of the labor force. CRPA did employ a few Japanese and their presence became a problem to this large company because of the government regulations governing Japanese residents at that time. Eight Japanese workers were living in the CRPA bunkhouse at the time of Pearl Harbor. Because of the sudden government regulations prohibiting Japanese from working on the waterfront, they could not work and could not leave so they simply stayed in the bunkhouse, waiting for the government to make up its mind what to do with them. Time passed and finally on April 27, 1942, CRPA notified the government that they needed the bunkhouse for the coming fishing season and would be forced to notify the Japanese to leave. Apparently, these eight were among the last Japanese in the area to leave for the government relocation camps in May of that year.

Local fishermen faced a multitude of new regulations to be followed if they were to continue salmon fishing in the Columbia River. Two large areas, one west of a line between Point Adams Coast Guard Station and McGowan, and the other in the vicinity of Tongue Point Naval Air Station were declared off limits for all fishing at any time which caused problems for many fishermen who had fished these areas all their lives.

Each fisherman had to get an identification card from the Coast Guard and, beginning on May 1st of that year, all fishing boats were inspected by the Coast Guard. All boats leaving or entering the Columbia River at any time had to notify the Coast Guard patrol boat during the daylight and, if they planned to cross the bar at night, they had to check in at the lightship first for identification and instructions. In addition, all boats including fishing boats had to get a license first from the U.S. Customs if they planned to fish at sea.

When price controls were put into effect, the fish packers were concerned because they felt that the prices set by the government were too low for efficient operations. They sent Tom Sandoz of CRPA to Washington, D.C. as a representative for all the local packing companies to plead for a higher ceiling price for the 1942 salmon pack.

Generally, however, the salmon and tuna packing industry fared well during World War II because they were called an essential industry, vital to the war effort, simply because they processed food. More than 66 per cent of all salmon canned was purchased by the armed forces but albacore tuna, not yet considered a staple food, was not needed by the Armed Forces Procurement Agency.

Graham Barbey, Henry's son, graduated from Stanford in 1941, and later became production manager for the Barbey Packing Co. He was unable to pass the eye examination for the navy, so he entered the army at Fort Lewis in 1942. It was decided by the government, however, that he was more important running a fish company than he was as a sergeant in the army so each year during the salmon season, he was sent home to help Henry Barbey run the cannery at Astoria. At the end of each season, he returned to Fort Lewis for the winter where he served at the induction center. At the end of the war, he was moved to the separation center at Fort Lewis. He said later, "I had the experience and the know-how so when I got that job, the first person I separated from the army was me."

The war actually did not have too much effect on the operation of the Barbey Packing Co. It had priorities on labor and other items. Whenever someone working at a cannery received a draft notice, the cannery would send a notice to the draft board and the employee was deferred until the end of the canning season.

In those days, Astoria was a serviceman's town with thousands of sailors from the Tongue Point Naval Base, the Port of Astoria Pier 2 Naval Base, the Navy Hospital, the Naval Airport, and soldiers from Fort Stevens and other army installations crowding its street daily. Even though many of these uniformed young men were just out of boot camp themselves, they went out of their way to make life miserable for any young local man not in uniform. The designation "4-F" was not a pleasant one to bear in those days so many of the young Astoria men went to college in other towns or enlisted voluntarily in one of the services rather than to spend the war years a virtual outcast in his own town.

"During the war, we had to have identification", Dorothy Caughey Johnson said. "I still have my Coast Guard pass. We went and applied for it, taking along our birth certificates. They took our pictures and apparently we were suppose to show these passes while coming and going on the waterfront but I cannot recall anyone ever checking mine".

However, because so many young people did leave for the various services and also because many Astorians went up to Portland to make what they called "big money" in the Kaiser ship yards, there was a shortage of production workers at all the local canneries and the call went out to housewives to go to work in the canneries as a part of the war effort.

Mrs. Ragna Tetlow, the author's mother, was one of the Astoria housewives who responded to this call. Her husband objected, saying there was no need for her to work but she went anyway. She had two stars up in her living room window to signify two sons serving with the armed forces, and the other son was in high school so there was no compelling reason to remain at home keeping house. She felt that she had to "do her bit".

She went to work at the Barbey Packing Co. plant and was put on the tuna line, beginning as a skinner and then working her way up to work as a packer. She had always been quick with her hands and caught on to the work quickly, soon becoming one of the best packers on the line. Naturally gregarious, she enjoyed the work and the opportunity to talk with others while working. She soon found others there like herself who had come to work to help the war effort but suddenly found that they enjoyed the work for its own sake.

She was able to put all of the money she earned into US War Bonds and, after the war, this extra money she had salted away partially paid for a long-awaited trip back to Norway to see relatives she had not seen since leaving Moss, Norway in 1914.

As soon as the war was over, she left the cannery work forever but, apparently, the unique experiences she had while working left a lasting impression on her. They probably gave her ego a lift when she found that she was able to hold her own in a real job. It was an experience shared by many other Astoria women of that time.

Even some of the military personnel stationed at nearby army and navy installations heeded the call for cannery workers. Riphath and Nethaneel Christensen were both stationed at an army base nearby. Nethaneel said later, "When we were at Camp Rilea, they were crying for help so when Rip and I were off work at the camp, we would go over there and work. We would put in two or three hours of work each time and the money earned sure added to our army pay."

Younger women also heeded the call to aid the war effort. Dorothy Caughey Johnson said, "I started at Barbey's when I was 17. That was about in 1943. I cleaned tuna fish. After school started, we would go down there at three in the afternoon and work until 8 or 9 at night. We made good money for kids — about 69 cents an hour, I think, but I didn't care much for cleaning tuna. They wanted us kids to work in the cannery to aid the war effort so we did.

"The following year I was called back and I operated the fish cutter and got to move around a bit. That year, we cleaned tuna clear into March. Then my friend who was a timekeeper left and I took over her job."

Dorothy Johnson stayed with the Barbey Packing Co. for many years working in the office. Morna Fitzgerald was the secretary then and J.D. Snell was the bookkeeper. Out in the cannery, Bill Ellis ran the boilers and the mechanic in charge of refrigeration was Clarence Oathes, while Buey Wong ran the Chinese gang.

"We had floor ladies," Dorothy said. "On the salmon side, we had Minnie Tark whose husband was the night watchman. They cleaned the office and lived in the apartment above the cannery. On the tuna side, Bea Scoffern was the floor lady for a few years. Graham Barbey was in the service at that time but he came and went, usually arriving in May and then leaving again for the army in November."

Dorothy Johnson remembered those war years at the Barbey cannery with pleasure. "We called him Mr. Barbey and we called Graham — Graham. We all did. I think Mr. Barbey had the respect of his employees and, if you worked for him and you were doing a good job, he left you alone. He was interested in everything and certainly kept an eye on everything. He was there when we worked late and he was there when we arrived in the morning.

"I remember one time the salmon cannery was shut down and I was walking through there to get into the tuna cannery and he came up to me and put his arm around me and told me what a good job I was doing. I was so pleased. He was like that — pleasant to everyone.

"The ladies got fresh uniforms once a week. I collected them on Fridays and put them in boxes for Troy Laundry to pick up. They wore white uniforms first and then they got blue ones. The women wore smocks and a cloth over their hair.

"I used to fix the coffee and order the hot rolls from the Home Bakery. I emptied the waste baskets and washed the windows in the office. There were holes in the office floor and I could see the water through them but when Graham returned from the army, he had the office remodeled. I think that Graham and his father disagreed on the necessity of doing that."

Dorothy continued to describe some of the details of her work at Barbeys. "I arrived there each morning at 7:30 and checked the skinners, and then the cleaners and packers who started an hour later but worked an hour longer in the evening. I checked them out at noon and back again, and I checked the warehouse gang to make sure they were all there. There were about twenty-five in the Chinese gang and then they had these eleven ladies on the salmon line. I also kept track of the Pillar Rock seining ground crew. There were about twenty-five men working out there.

"The war ended about four in the afternoon and I always blew the whistle and I ran out and asked Bill if I could blow that whistle. They were blowing all over town. Everyone quit work then and went home." Dorothy Johnson smiled. "That was a great day."

The war did effect the canning production of the Barbey Packing Co., however. As the war continued, annual production of both salmon and tuna fell drastically due to war problems.

1942 - 20,210 cases salmon

18,000 cases albacore tuna

1943 - 10,182 cases salmon

9,075 cases albacore tuna

1944 - 6,027 cases salmon

4,219 cases albacore tuna

1945 - 4,371 cases salmon

2,680 cases albacore tuna

Henry Barbey and other members of the Barbey family followed the war news from the Pacific area with more interest than usual because of the high-level activities of Henry's younger brother Daniel who by this time was an admiral in the United States Navy and was frequently mentioned in the military dispatches.

Dan was younger than Henry and had always looked up to him for guidance and help. According to his widow Katherine Barbey of Olympia who was interviewed in 1986

Henry and Ethel Barbey with Henry's brother Admiral Daniel Barbey on their winter vacation at Beverly Hills.

when she was ninety-three years old, "Dan admired his brother Henry. He said to me that of all the men he ever met, Henry was the best. There is nobody like Henry," he said.

After graduating from Annapolis, Dan Barbey spent the rest of his life in the Navy, receiving assignments to various posts while working his way up through the ranks. He was at Portland in 1936 as the commander of a destroyer flotilla and took the time to travel down to Astoria to visit his brother. His wife Katherine accompanied him.

She told of an incident that happened at the cannery which illustrates the difference between the two brothers' methods of getting things done. "Dan and Henry were touring the cannery when they came across one of the workers who was supposed to be hosing down the floor but who had fallen asleep at the job with the water still pouring from the hose. Dan was furious and would have awakened him and reprimanded or fired him but Henry simply went over to the faucet and turned off the water. It was subtle. He knew that the man would awaken and wonder who did it, and then he would figure out that it had been the boss and would be scared to death and would never do it again.

"They were different kinds of men but both of them would have succeeded in anything they did."

She first met and married Daniel Barbey in 1928. "Dan took me down to Astoria then and I met Henry for the first time. Graham was just a tot then. Very independent and always laughing. His mother, Ethel, was serious and I can remember her saying, 'Now, Graham, there are two kinds of people: people who succeed and people who fail. I want you to succeed and you must do your lessons.' "

"That didn't upset him at all. Graham always had a nice disposition."

"When I married Dan," Mrs. Barbey said, "he was a lieutenant commander so I never did have to go through the junior naval ranks with him. I was lucky in that respect."

After being commissioned an ensign in the navy after his graduation from Annapolis in 1912, he was assigned as a junior officer to the USS *California* in June of that year, and to the USS *Lawrence* in 1914, the USS *Annapolis* in 1916, and the USS *Stevens* in 1918.

Dan Barbey's naval career followed the general lines of all naval officers moving up through the ranks towards the admirals' stars. After World War I, he was the naval port officer at Cardiff, Wales in 1919, and at the US naval headquarters in London in that same year. In 1920, he was named commander of the U.S. naval forces in Turkey.

He returned to sea duty then, serving on the USS *Capella* and the USS *Oklahoma* in 1922, the USS *Cincinnati* in 1925, and the USS *Ramapo* in 1927. In 1931, he was commanding the USS *Lea,* and in 1935 was a first lieutenant on the USS

Admiral Daniel Barbey in 1944. (Photo courtesy National Archives.)

New York and later commanding officer on the USS *Ramapo*. In 1940, he was named commanding officer of the battleship USS *New York*.

During these years in the navy, he became known as an ardent student of naval strategy and possessed the capacity to innovate, to understand, and to integrate new ideas into the pattern of naval warfare. In May 1942, Dan Barbey was put in charge of the first Amphibious Warfare Section of the navy, charged with the development of landing craft and the tactics of their employment. From this work came ideas for the many odd landing craft used later for the amphibious landings in the Pacific area.

Having worked with the development of these landing craft, it was logical that he was assigned to put these ideas into actual practice and in June 1943, his landing crafts had their first trial in actual combat when Kiriwina and Woodlark were successfully occupied by American forces.

Following that first landing, he participated in sixty-two major amphibious assaults. In all, Admiral Barbey's command landed more than one million soldiers and marines, together with more than 1,500,000 tons of equipment and supplies. It was his Seventh Amphibious Force that led the invasions of Leyte Gulf and the Lingayen Gulf. During this time, Admiral Dan Barbey became known as "Uncle Dan the Amphibious Man".

Admiral Barbey accepted the surrender of the Japanese command at Seoul, Korea, after he landed army troops at Inchon, Korea, at the end of World War II.

After the war, he was sent to the Far East as chairman of a Joint Military Board to report on the strategic requirements of that area. Following that, he was named commandant of the Tenth Naval District and commander of the Caribbean Sea Frontier in 1947, and commandant of the 13th Naval District in 1950. He retired from the navy in 1951.

Admiral Barbey held many medals and decorations including the Navy Cross, Distinguished Service Medal with a gold star, the Army Distinguished Service Medal and the Legion of Merit.

He was also awarded the rank of Grand Officer in the Order of Orange Nassau with Swords (Netherlands), Honorary Commander of the Order of the British Empire, Grand Order of the Cloud and Banner (China), Commander of the Order of the Liberator (Venezuela), Order of Merit Juan Pable Duarte, Degree of Great Cross, Silver Plaque and Order of Christopher Columbus, Degree of Great Cross, Silver Plaque (Dominican Republic).

Admiral Daniel Barbey receiving the Navy Cross in 1943. (Photo courtesy National Archives.)

Admiral Dan Barbey once gave Graham Barbey some good advice. Graham was an enlisted man in the army and went to see his Uncle Dan about taking officers training. Dan asked him if he planned to stay in the army and when Graham said that he wasn't, Dan said, "Then don't do it."

That wasn't the first time that Dan Barbey had given Graham good advice. After he had graduated from high school, Graham applied for admission to Stanford, Harvard, and Yale, and was accepted by all of them. When Dan heard about it, he said to Graham, "You're going to stay on the West Coast so you should have friends on the West Coast. Go to Stanford."

"It was good advice," Graham said, "and I followed it. I was graduated from Stanford in 1941 and found that what my uncle said had been true. It is good to have friends on the West Coast when you work there."

The Barbey Packing Co. weathered those war years and emerged in good condition but the times were changing. It was obvious that the fisheries on the Columbia River were declining due to overfishing, pollution, dam construction, and other factors, and if additional salmon were to be found, it would have to be elsewhere. Puget Sound and the Washington fisheries were all tied up but north of Washington lay Alaska, a territory still open to new enterprises.

In Alaska, licenses were issued to cannery ships which moved from area to area wherever the salmon were most plentiful. Building a cannery in Alaska or even buying an existing one would be too expensive but if a suitable ship could be found which could be converted into a floating cannery, it would be possible for the Barbeys to move into that area for a new supply of salmon.

The end of World War II suddenly created an opportunity to get such a ship. The government had set up the War Assets Department for the purpose of liquidating all the surplus ships, buildings, food, and other wartime commodities not used during the war and which were of no further use to a nation now at peace.

Henry and Graham Barbey decided to look for a suitable ship from that source and found two naval ships located at Nordlund, Washington, either of which could be converted into a floating cannery. The *Vent* and the *Valve* were large tugs, 183 feet long with a 37 foot beam and a 13 foot depth. They were each equipped with four 440 H.P. Cooper Bessemer diesels, working through diesel-electric drives. They both had the latest in navigational equipment including radar, depth sounders, direction finders, and each cruised at fifteen knots.

The Barbey Packing Co. put in the highest bid on the ships and won the right to buy either or both of them so the *Vent* was chosen as it was brand new and had never been to sea other than on a shakedown cruise in the Seattle area. The *Vent* was towed to Astoria by the Foss Tug and Barge Co. and moored at Pier 2 at the Port of Astoria, within walking distance of the Barbey Packing Co. cannery.

To buy the *Vent* and operate the proposed new Alaskan venture, a new corporation was formed in 1948 when the Oregon Pacific Fisheries, Inc. was organized by the Barbeys, and incorporated for $100,000, with all stock owned by the Barbey family. Graham Barbey was elected president, Anne M. Barbey, Graham's wife, became the vice-president, and Ethel G. Barbey was named secretary-treasurer.

Graham Barbey had refrigeration engineers draw plans for converting the *Vent,* now renamed *Oregon Pacific,* into a floating cannery and also into a freezer ship so that the salmon could be brought to Astoria for canning.

Unfortunately, the Alaska laws were changed just about that time causing the venture to fall through. The salmon packers in Alaska had been unhappy with the success of the freezer ships and pushed a law through the Alaska legislature which stipulated that the Alaska Department of Fisheries could license a floating cannery or freezer ship so that it could operate in only one area, just like a shorebound cannery. This new law took away their advantage of mobility and made the expense of converting a ship into a floating cannery or freezer ship economically unsound.

Bowing to the inevitable, the Barbey Packing Co. gave up the idea of converting the *Oregon Pacific* and sold it to a buyer in Alaska who put it into service as a tug boat operating between Seattle and Alaska.

Times were changing now and Henry Barbey was getting older, was tired, and was ready to take it easier. He had been troubled with diabetes since the age of fifty and, even though he kept himself in good physical condition, was almost ready to hand the reins of management over to his son, Graham.

A new era was coming for the Barbey Packing Co. of Astoria.

Chapter 20

HENRY BARBEY'S FINAL YEARS

In the early part of 1948, customers, employees and others who had been dealing with the Barbey Packing Co. received the following notice:

The writer wishes to advise that, as of May 1, 1948, the business of the Barbey Packing Company has been taken over by the Barbey Packing Corporation, an Oregon corporation.

My son, Graham J. Barbey, is President and Manager of the Corporation. I am Vice President, and will continue to take an active interest in the affairs of the Corporation.

The Barbey Packing Company has always been an unincorporated company. The stock of the Barbey Packing Corporation is entirely owned by myself and family, and the Corporation will continue the policy of the Barbey Packing Company.

At this time I wish to express my appreciation for our pleasant business relationships with you in the past, and my hope for their continuance.

BARBEY PACKING CORPORATION
by H.J. Barbey

As the Barbey Packing Corporation, the firm was capitalized at $200,000 divided into 2,000 shares, all owned by members of the Barbey family. In addition to the election of Graham Barbey as president, and Henry J. Barbey as vice-president, Ethel G. Barbey was named secretary and treasurer.

On April 23, 1947, Graham Barbey had married Ann Murray of Tacoma, daughter of Lowell Thomas Murray, owner of the West Fork Timber Company of Tacoma, Washington. Miss Murray was a graduate of Annie Wright Seminary, and Vassar College.

Graham, Ethel and Henry Barbey at home for Christmas at their Astoria residence.

After a honeymoon in California, the young couple returned to Astoria to live in their new home on Coxcomb Drive.

In 1948, Henry Barbey would reach his 65th birthday and he was tired. He had been in the salmon packing industry for almost forty years and had been one of the major figures dominating that industry during those years when changes swept away huge portions of it. He had seen the fall of the fish traps and fishwheels. The heyday of the seining grounds was over for all practical purposes although seining continued into the early 1950s. Most of the salmon coming in to the canneries now were caught by gillnetters and the Barbey Packing Co. had never been one of the major users of gillnet salmon during the 1920s and 1930s. Henry had kept away from the sometimes costly practice of financing gillnetters, depending more on other sources of salmon.

No, the salmon industry had changed and it was time to step down and turn his salmon packing plant over to his son Graham who was younger and ready to guide the Barbey Packing Co. through the coming difficult years of change.

Graham said this later about his father: "It was very difficult for him to not do anything after he turned the company over to me. He would wander around the cannery, watching production. I kept an office there for him and he used that when he was in town. He and my mother would go to California for the winter and they went on several cruises but his real home was the cannery and he found it very difficult to stay away from it for any length of time."

"He was always good-humored during those days", Graham said. "He had a great sense of humor and loved to play jokes on our family. I can recall once when the family was all sitting in the living room of our Astoria house, my father was reading the local paper and suddenly announced that the paper said he had bought the Astoria Hotel and planned to completely remodel it and then operate it. All of us looked up, amazed, while he pretended to read the balance of the non-existent article to the assembled family. Finally, we realized that he was kidding and went back to our own reading but the incident was typical of the kind of jokes he loved to pull on his friends and family."

Henry's niece, Caroline Ivey Kelley, said this about Henry Barbey: "I always thought of him as being reserved also but he was such fun. He told more cute stories and he had such a wonderful sense of humor. I remember that so well. I can remember him as smiling continually. Of course, Uncle Dan was that way too. He had a wonderful sense of humor. They both did."

Dorothy Johnson laughed as she remembered one humorous thing Henry Barbey did in 1948. "I think it was in the spring of that year when we had the big earthquake here," she said. "I was in the cannery at the time and the building was rocking back and forth on its piling foundation, kind of like a boat in rough water. At the height of it, Mr. Barbey stuck his head out of the office door and said to me, "Dorothy, make those boys stop whatever they are doing. They're shaking the building so much I can't work."

When Henry Barbey turned the cannery over to Graham, he gave him some good advice. "When the warehouse is empty, that is the time to sell the company. You don't sell at the bottom, you sell at the top."

Even though Henry Barbey kept an office at the cannery and was usually around during the packing season, Graham still needed help in running the cannery so he hired other people to take over under him. One of these was Jim Ferguson, now a Seattle businessman.

"I started at Barbey's on June 15, 1960", he said. "Henry Barbey was retired but he still came to the plant every day. I was with them from 1960 to 1964 as a kind of college student in the summer. I would come back in June and leave in September. When I came back here, I had two terms of college left and so Graham paid me for nine months work and then subsidized me — gave me $500 a month which was more or less a scholarship when I wasn't even working there so I could finish my schooling. Now, there aren't many people like that who would take a young guy and help him just out of the goodness of their hearts but that's the way the Barbeys were. Really fine people.

"Graham brought me in as production manager and then I was the general manager after a couple of years. I was there five years and then I left in '69, mainly because I felt that there was no future on the river. It wasn't anything the Barbeys did because they couldn't have been better. They always went out of their way to be nice to me.

"Henry was such a proud man — always stood high. Very straight because he had such a good posture. And Mrs. Barbey was such a lady. She was always a very pleasant person. There were no problems of any kind with her."

Actually, Henry Barbey had never been socially involved with the communities he lived in, preferring to devote all of his time to his business. He did belong to the Astoria Golf and Country Club, of course, because of his interest in playing golf, and he was a member of the Astoria Chamber of Commerce. He was also invited to join the University Club of Portland, even though he was not a college graduate. This was an honor not offered to many.

In these organizations, however, he never played an active part. He was a member but never held office in any of them, preferring to devote his time to his beloved packing enterprises.

Julia Barbey, mother of Henry Barbey.

Most of the other members of the Barbey family lived in Portland. Henry's father John Barbey had died in 1930 and his mother Julia Chloupek Barbey died in 1942 but his sisters in 1948 were all living in Portland. The oldest, Blanche, married Tom Reed of Reed Brothers, Tailors, a top custom tailor shop in Portland. According to Henry's sister Frances, Henry had all of his suits tailored there because he was always very particular about the quality and cut of the suits he wore and felt that Reed Bros. was the only tailoring shop in Portland that could satisfy him. The Reeds had two children, Barbara and Dorothy. Blanche Rose Barbey Reed died in 1969.

Two of the Barbey girls, Caroline Helen Barbey and Frances Grace Barbey never married. Frances taught school at Catlin

School in Portland for many years and was a counselor, both at Pomona College in Clairmont, California, and later at Lake Oswego High School where she also taught history. She is retired at the present time and lives at Terwilliger Plaza in Portland.

The career of Henry's brother Daniel has been discussed in a previous chapter. He retired from the US Navy in 1951 and died in 1969. His widow Katherine, now lives in Olympia, Washington.

Henry's other sister, Hazel, married Ralph Ivey, Deputy City Auditor of Portland for many years. They had two children, Richard and Carolyn.

During these years, Henry Barbey became a grandfather. Graham and his wife Anne had two daughters, Anita and Helena. Today, Helena lives in California and is married to Gary Coover, vice-president of Kidder Peabody in San Francisco. They have two boys, Graham and Gary Jr. Anita was married to Dr. Roland Bennetts of Portland, Oregon. Both Anita and Helena graduated from Stanford University.

"The Barbeys had about 125 gillnetters fishing for them up and down the river to Bonneville", Jim Ferguson said. "they financed quite a few of them but some of those fishermen in the 1960s were very difficult to get along with. I can remember once we had a big storm. It was raining sideways and blowing, and the watchman called me to tell me that one of the gillnet boats tied up at the dock was sinking.

"I called this fellow and told him that his boat was sinking," Jim laughed at the memory. "Now, here is a man we had loaned probably $1500 to on a boat that was worth maybe $2,000. We used to pay all of his fuel bills, groceries — all kinds of things so after he heard about his boat, he said, 'Blankety blank, it's your boat. You go down and pump it out.' He then hung up the phone.

"I should have let the boat go down and let him miss the season but I didn't. I went down to the boat with the watchman, dragged a battery over to it and pumped the boat out, getting thoroughly wet and miserable in the process. I wasn't very happy about that deal.

"Later in that same season, I went over to the receiving scows at one time and here was this same guy — he was a good fisherman — with the biggest load of silvers I had ever seen. Our scow was standing right there and he was delivering his fish to New England Fish Co. for cash."

Jim Ferguson went on with his story: "I went over to him and asked him if he didn't think he should deliver his silvers to Barbey. He knew that I could take his boat away if he didn't so he started to give them to our scow with his tail between his legs. That's the kind of guy that Barbey had to deal with in those days. Not all of them, of course, but you tend to remember the ones who were jerks.

"What happened to the Barbey's operation," Jim Ferguson said, "was not anything that the Barbeys did wrong but they were a victim of circumstances because of the dwindling fish runs. When I first went to work there in 1960, we had about a hundred days of gillnetting each year but when I left in 1969-70, we were down to about 30 days. It's very hard to cover your fixed costs when you have such a low volume.

"Another problem which came up was the sudden growth of the fresh fish market. Barbey canned salmon but the price was set by some guy sitting over at Megler with a pickup truck who bought a thousand or two pounds of salmon for a nickle or a dime more than the packers were paying. He would set the price for the entire river. Barbey had a high overhead but the man in the pickup truck had very little overhead. He just delivered his salmon to a couple of outlets in Portland. If the packers had to pay what he was paying for fresh salmon, there was no way they could make a profit. Cash buyers were a very great problem to the packers."

An examination of the annual pack of albacore tuna and salmon by the Barbey Packing Corp. vividly shows the declining pack during these years.

1949 - Salmon	-	3,500 cases
Albacore	-	9,900 cases
1950 - Salmon	-	8,000 cases
Albacore	-	10,000 cases
1951 - Salmon	-	11,500 cases
Albacore	-	8,000 cases

```
1952 - Salmon    -   9,000 cases
       Albacore  -   6,700 cases
1953 - Salmon    -  10,400 cases
       Albacore  -   6,500 cases
1954 - Salmon    -  10,000 cases
       Albacore  -   8,000 cases
1955 - Salmon    -  10,000 cases
       Albacore  - No albacore tuna pack
1956 - Salmon    -  10,000 cases
1957 - Salmon    -  10,000 cases
1958 - Salmon    -  12,500 cases
1959 - Salmon    -  10,500 cases
1960 - Salmon    -   7,500 cases
1961 - Salmon    -   8,000 cases
1962 - Salmon    -   8,500 cases
1963 - Salmon    -   2,500 cases
1964 - Salmon    -   4,500 cases
```

"Another problem that the Barbeys had," Jim Ferguson said, "was that they always packed top quality fish. I used to go to Seattle to be a judge when the salmon packers had these meetings. They took the labels and codes off the cans so no one knew who canned them and then we judged the quality of the salmon in those cans. There were about twenty-five of us judges and the Barbey fish always scored very, very high. But packing top quality fish is always more expensive. Even so, the Barbeys never did cut down on quality."

Henry Barbey continued to show an interest in the Barbey Packing Corp. right up to the end of his life. Even though Graham was running the show, he managed to be down at the plant as often as possible, and was always interested in all of the operations.

In his eightieth year, Henry Barbey developed cancer. He was sent to the Columbia Hospital in Astoria but remained there for only two days before insisting on returning to his home. "If I'm going to die," he said, "I want to die at home."

On February 9, 1964, Henry Barbey died at the age of 80.

Chapter 21

THE LAST DAYS OF THE
BARBEY PACKING CO.

Graham Barbey took over the reins of the Barbey Packing Corporation in 1948. At this time, the canning of salmon and the canning of albacore tuna were the important economic factors in the Astoria area, but this situation was to soon change as the number of commercial fishing days allowed were curtailed each year by the joint action of the Oregon Fish Commission and the Washington Department of Fisheries.

It was soon evident by the yearly pack figures that the production of albacore tuna had surpassed the salmon canning on the Columbia River.

In 1970, Graham Barbey hired Joseph Bakkensen, Western Regional Sales Manager for Bumble Bee Seafoods, to become general manager of the Barbey Packing Corp. Henry Barbey had been gone six years and a new era was developing on the Columbia River.

By this time, the canning of salmon and the canning of tuna had been augmented by the fresh and frozen salmon business and the large volume of tuna being shipped to California to Ralston Purina by the Barbey Packing Corporation.

Joe Bakkensen said later, "Barbey then was mostly into gillnet fish — salmon, sturgeon, and a lot of shad roe. We were unloading albacore for Van Camp. We were the biggest in shad roe and Graham had developed a good market, probably more private labels with the old S.S. Pierce label and S & W, and Sexton. Then in 1974, the American Can Company had the last half-pound oval can machines in the United States but decided it was not worth the effort to make those cans so they sold it to some outfit in Mexico and quit making oval cans. I heard about this and bought up all the oval cans they had left. We had about a four year supply on hand then."

The gross sales of Barbey Packing by 1973 were the highest in the history of the company, hitting approximately $20 million. Graham Barbey had made Joe Bakkensen vice president as well as general manager of the corporation by this time.

Now, there were only four major packing companies left on the lower Columbia River: Barbey Packing Corp., Bumble Bee Seafoods, Union Fishermens Cooperative Packing Co., and Point Adams Packing Co.

In 1971 Graham Barbey had a bout with cancer from which he subsequently had a complete recovery. The doctors advised him in that year that if he lived five years, the cancer operation would be successful. He therefore decided he didn't want to leave the Barbey Packing Corp. to Mrs. Barbey to operate if anything happened to him, so he started looking for a possible sale.

Both Ralston Purina in St. Louis, Missouri, owned by Van Camp Seafoods on Terminal Island, California, packers of Chicken of the Sea tuna, and Westgate Sun Harbor, located in San Diego, California, packers of Breast of Chicken tuna, showed an interest in the purchase of the Barbey Packing Corp. and entered into negotiations with Graham Barbey, who, with his wife and two children, owned 100% of the stock.

At this point, Joe Bakkensen approached Graham Barbey and inquired if he might be given an opportunity to work up a proposal to purchase the company. After being given an affirmative answer, Bakkensen put together a group of three prominent Astorians; himself, Ted Bugas, vice-president of Castle & Cooke, parent company of Bumble Bee Seafoods, and United States Congressman Wendell Wyatt. The three businessmen, with the backing of the United States National Bank of Oregon, made a successful offer and on May 1, 1974, the headlines of the *Daily Astorian* read, "Wyatt, Bugas, Bakkensen Buy Out Largest Columbia Salmon Cannery." At this point in time, Bumble Bee Seafoods was the largest cannery but the records show that their volume was in tuna and fresh and frozen salmon on the Columbia River whereas the Barbey Packing Corporation put up the largest canned salmon pack.

Barbey Packing Corporation's new management was an aggressive group who purchased Union Fishermens Cooperative Packing Corp in 1975. When the Barbey sign went up on the Union Fish's cannery buildings, many old-time gillnetters must have turned over in their graves.

Joe Bakkensen said, "After Union Fish closed down, we remembered that they had a big freezer there and, since we needed freezer space, we wanted to lease that. In the process, we got into negotiations and found that they would like to get rid of the whole thing so we finally got all of their properties in the State of Oregon. New freezer plants, trucks, forklifts, two or three canning lines which we sold off, ice making equipment — they had a new fifty ton flake ice machine they hadn't even hooked up yet which came with it."

"So we took it over, put in the shrimp plant and moved over there, closing down the old Barbey cannery at the Port of Astoria. We used it for buying tuna and the fishermen stored nets there but canning in that plant had come to an end."

Bakkensen reported that their big move was to add a large shrimp operation in 1976 and their gross sales in 1977 rose to $26 million. He stated that in 1976, they handled 23,000 tons of albacore tuna and 7 million pounds of shrimp, then worth about $12 million.

"We had a big year. The tuna fishermen were all mad at Bumble Bee so we had maybe 97% of the tuna that was unloaded there that year. In fact, the Bumble Bee boats were coming to our cannery to unload to us and Bumble Bee would back up their trucks to our door. Elmore cannery would not have boats being unloaded and these guys would wait two or three days to unload with us and we put it all into the Bumble Bee trucks because they had contracts with the fishermen to sell them their fish. We got paid $85 a ton that year unloading and we did close to seven million pounds of shrimp that year with six machines. Bumble Bee, with twelve machines, beat us by only two million pounds. On river salmon, we were Number One."

This was the height of the Barbey Packing Corporation. Joe Bakkensen sold his interest in 1978 to Peter Pan Seafoods, which was owned by the Bristol Bay Native Corporation. It later sold its ownership of Peter Pan in Astoria, Seattle, and Alaska to a Japanese trading company Nichiro Gyogyo K.K., which closed the operation on the Columbia River in 1981.

Since that time, the Port of Astoria has purchased both the original Barbey Packing Corporation buildings and property on Pier 1 of the Port of Astoria, and the property and buildings which was once the Union Fishermens Cooperative Packing Co. Both of these buildings have now been demolished.

So it is all gone now, the buildings, the boats, the men, and most of the fish, but the history of the Columbia River and the Lower Columbia area will always include tributes to those intrepid men who gambled their lives and fortunes on the river salmon and the ocean albacore tuna. These men built an industry which employed thousands of men and women for more than a hundred years, and provided one of the world's finest foods to the people of all nations.

Henry Barbey of the Barbey Packing Co. will always be included as one of the early-day pioneers and also as one of the last of the Columbia River salmon and tuna packers because he was a leader of the industry almost from the beginning and was there at the end. His career spanned the best and most exciting days of the Columbia River salmon industry, and he will be remembered for his many contributions to that industry.

The wonderful top quality spring pack Columbia River Fancy Chinook Salmon is no longer available from the Barbey Packing Corporation, but pictures, labels, and artifacts from the cannery are on display at the Columbia River Maritime Museum in Astoria where Mr. and Mrs. Graham Barbey donated the money to build the fisheries section in honor of Henry Barbey.

INDEX